Stefan Salinas

The Concert and the Closet

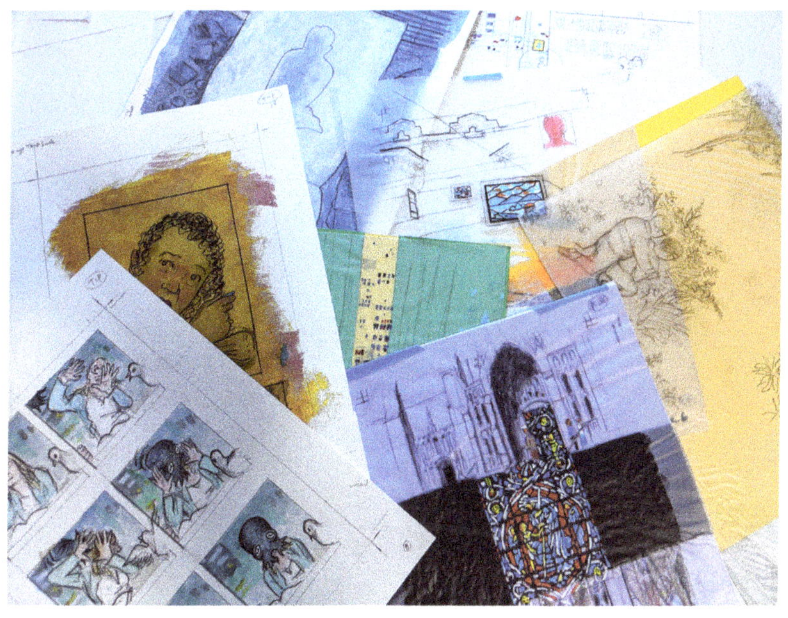

October Recital

———

A Parade in June

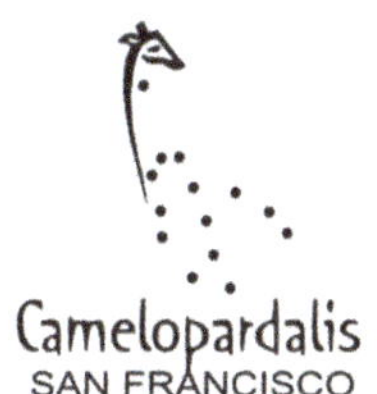

Camelopardalis
SAN FRANCISCO

October Recital first published in 2011.
   Special thanks to the editor: Jack Ronan.
   Thank you Sara Hron, Kelsey Walsh, Eric Langhirt and Michael Higgins.
   English translation of Gustav Mahler's song *Die zwei blauen Augen von meinen Schatz* is printed with kind permission from Emily Ezust, the translator.

A Parade in June first published in 2012.
   Special thanks to the editor: Jack Ronan.
   Thank you Donal Godfrey, Stephen S., and those who helped me find a seat at the banquet table.
   Quote on page 80 is from:
   Godfrey, Donal. *Gays and Grays* (Maryland: Lexington Books, 2007), 55

Camelopardalis / Stefan Salinas
PO Box 470041, San Francisco, CA 94147 USA

https://www.stefansalinas.com

Printed on acid-free paper by IngramSpark in the USA/UK/Australia.

In memory of Stephanie Martin,
a true lover of the arts.

———————

To the LGBTQ+
community of faith.

A friend stopped by the shop
to drop off a gift "for the apartment.
I gotta go — I'm double parked."

"Thank you," I said, "Thank you
for this. We'll have coffee
soon, yes?"

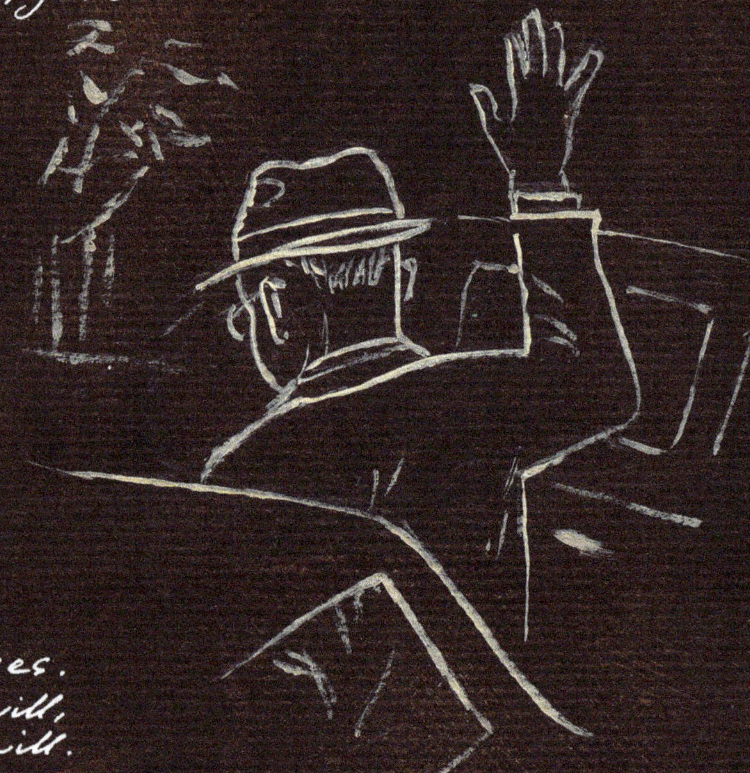

"yes, yes.
We will,
we will.

Please be
patient with me.
I'm still in darkness."

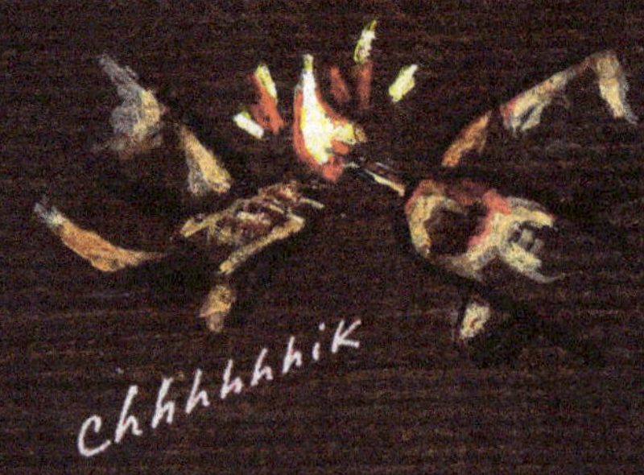

I'm still in darkness.

Let me tell you
about a day
I had last October...

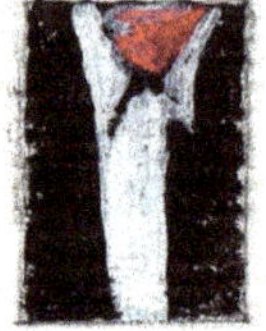

Eric announces Online
    that he's in a group recital today.
    He's my choir buddy and
            a close friend.

—   "I will sing about
            deep despair."

"I walked here and there —
yesterday pondering my own
    deep despair,"
Says Millicent, "still
        with me this morning."

October Recital
by
Stefan Salinas
Camelopardalis • San Francisco

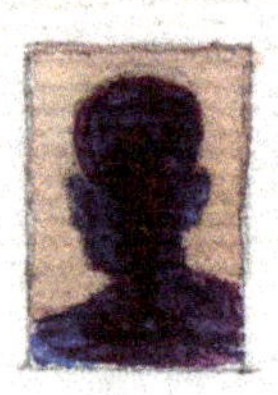

—   I reply,
    "Let it lift like the morning fog;
    It may return at dusk,
    but give yourself the day. Take a
    walkabout. Attend
        a friend's recital!"

I hop over to the library, then to a
Café near the Conservatory of music,
-pondering Millicent's statement from
this morning... it's as if there's a
thin red line connecting my
heart to her word
"despair."

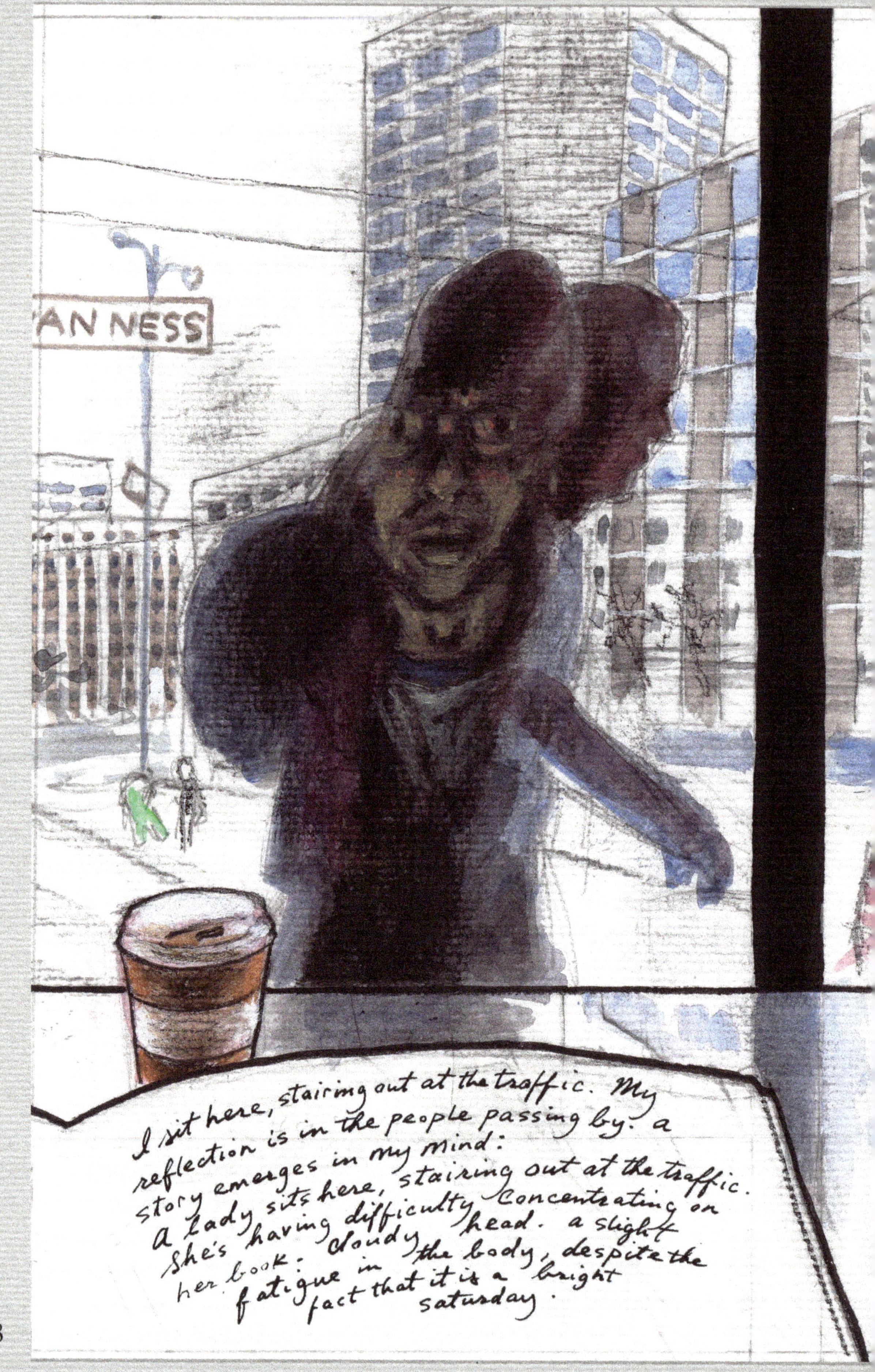
AN NESS
I sit here, stairing out at the traffic. My
reflection is in the people passing by. a
story emerges in my mind:
A lady sits here, stairing out at the traffic.
She's having difficulty concentrating on
her book. Cloudy head. a slight
fatigue in the body, despite the
fact that it is a bright
saturday.

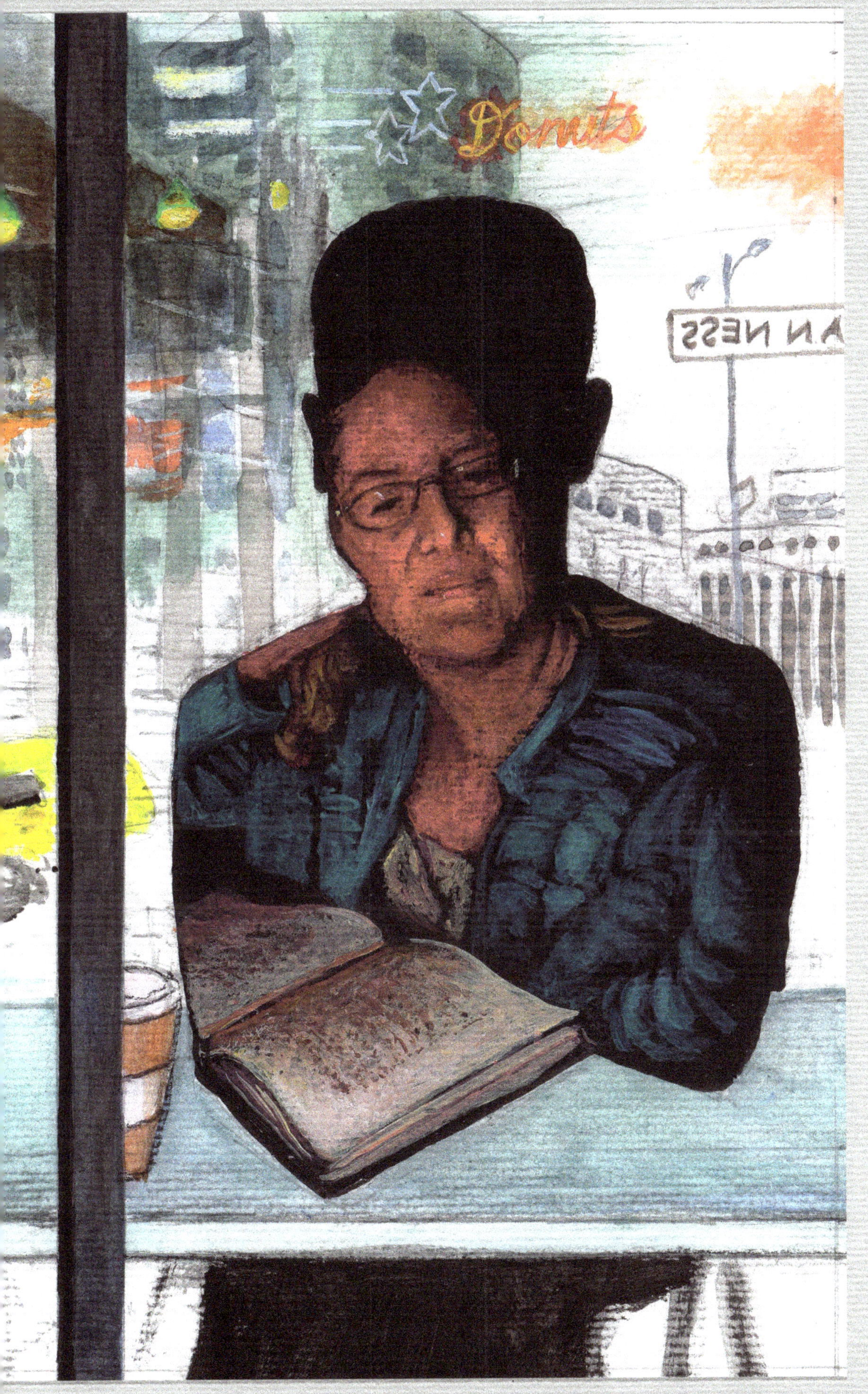
Donuts
AN NESS

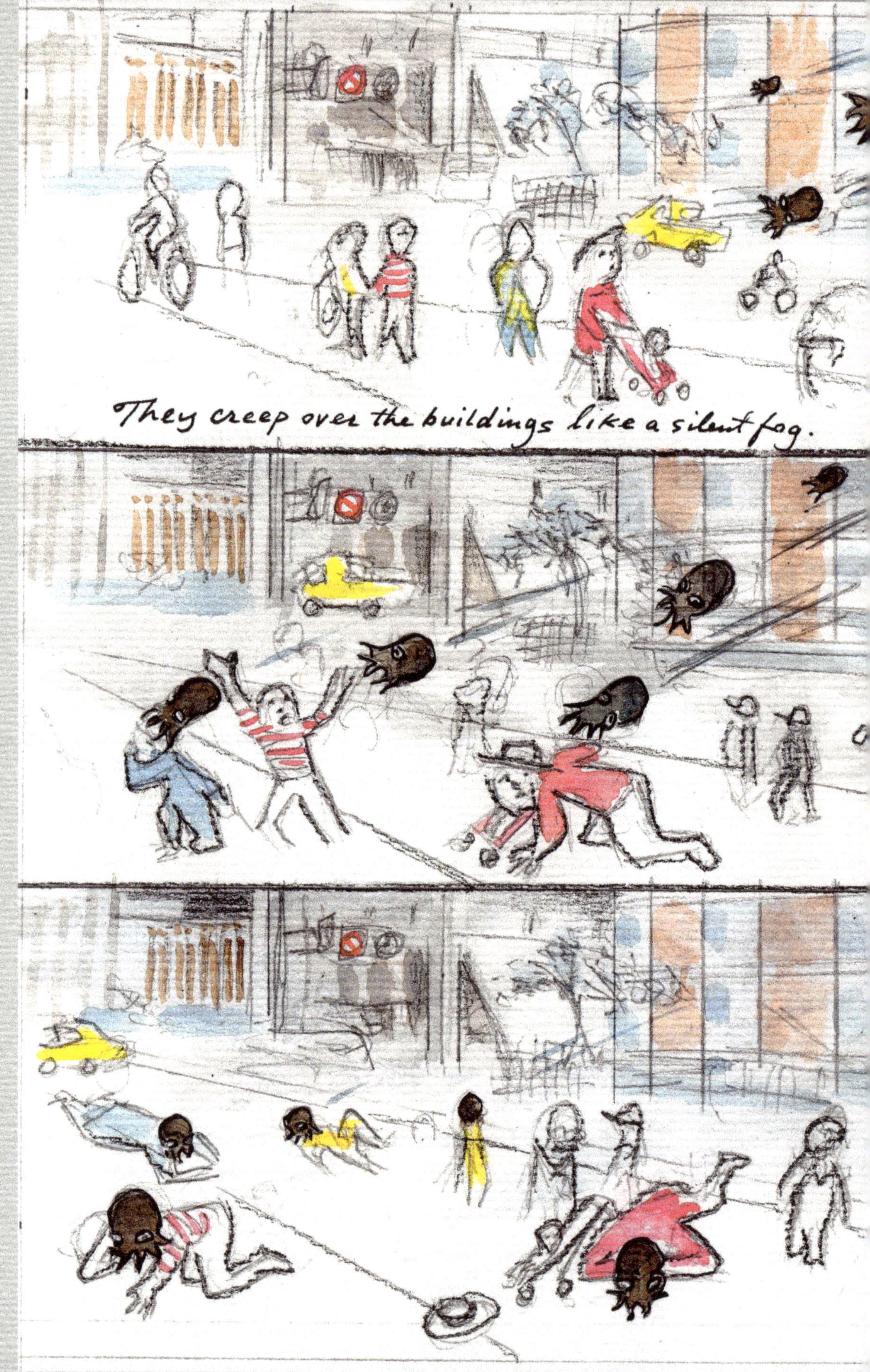

They creep over the buildings like a silent fog.

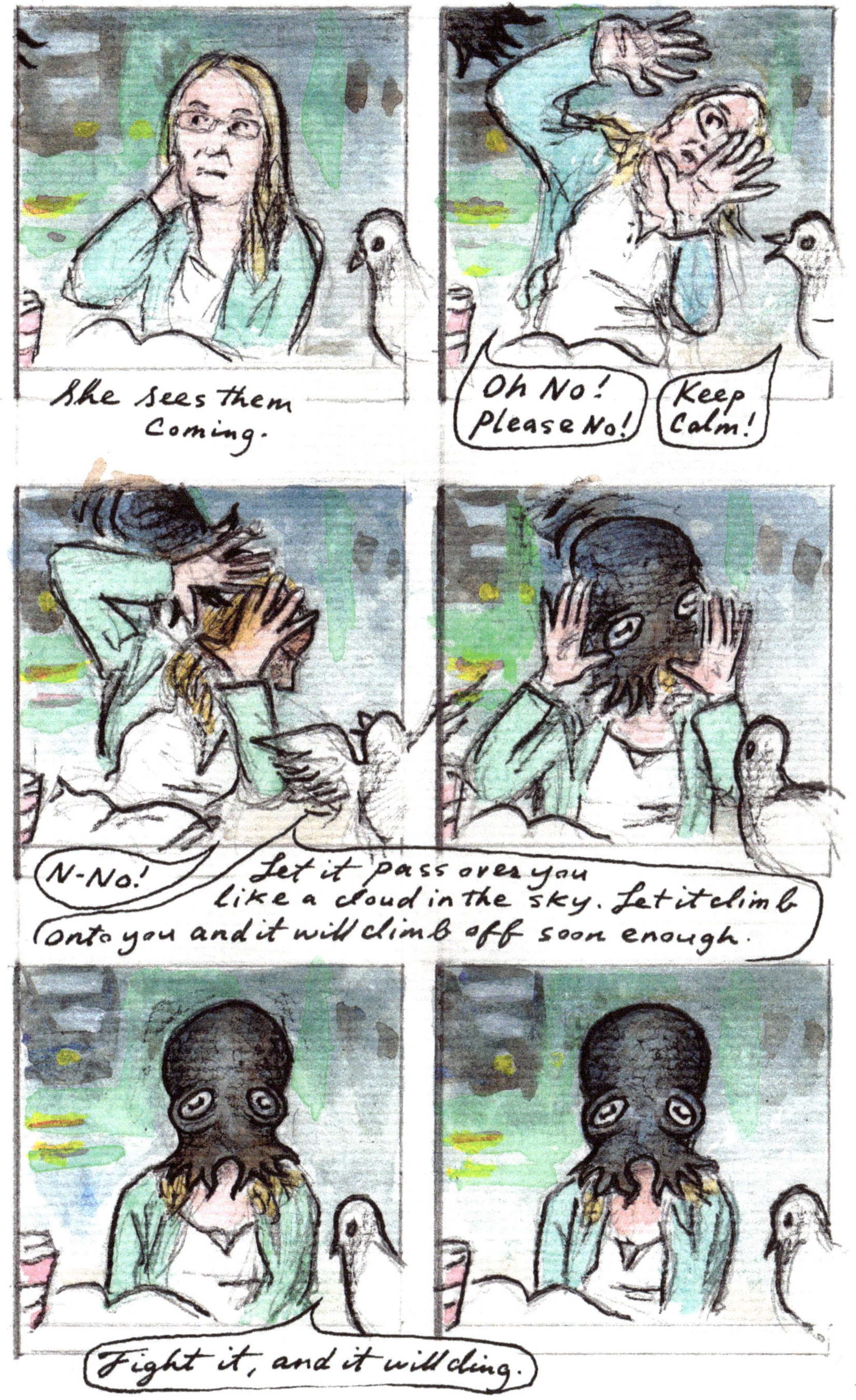

She sees them coming.
Oh No! Please No!
Keep Calm!
N-No!
Let it pass over you like a cloud in the sky. Let it climb onto you and it will climb off soon enough.
Fight it, and it will cling.

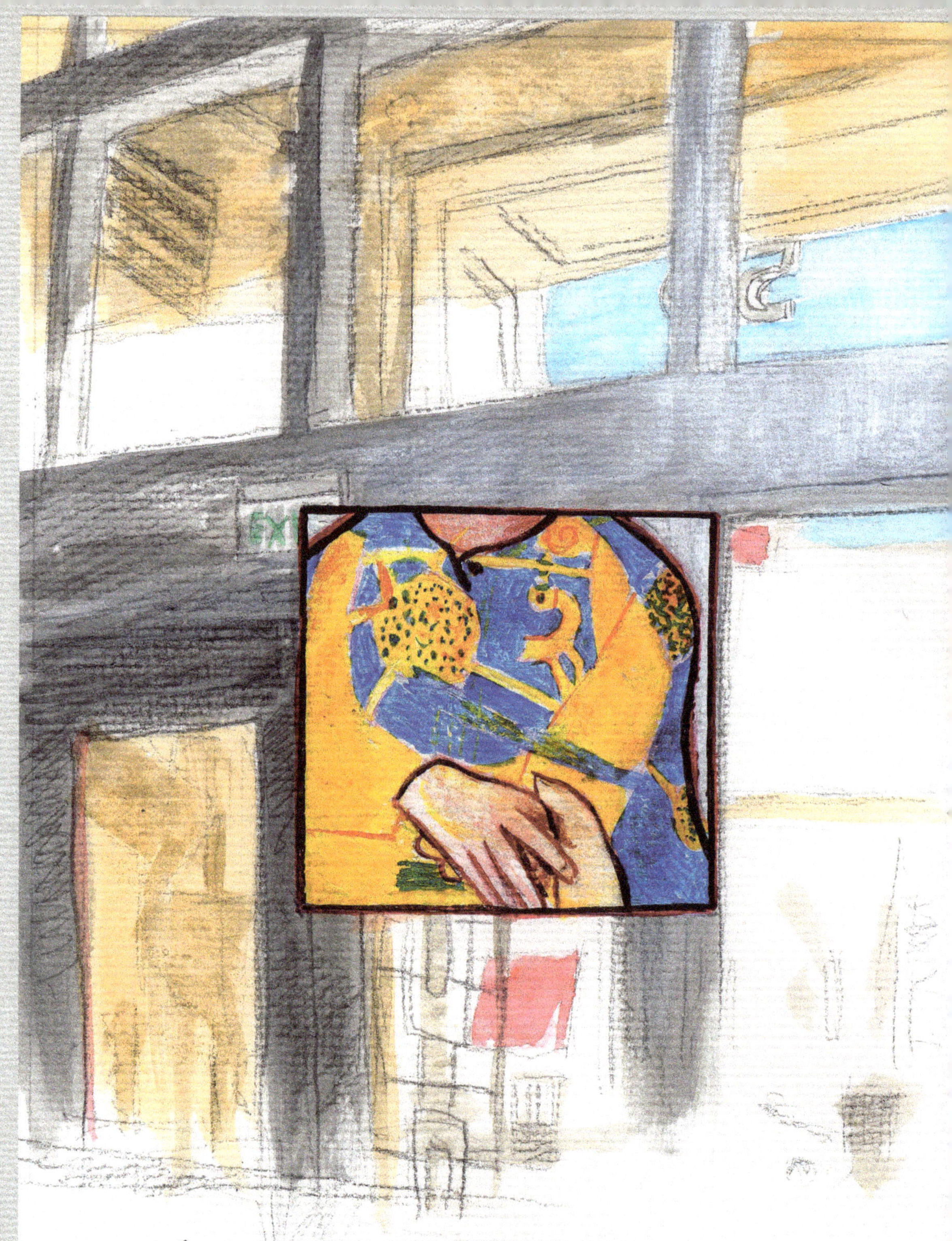

I move on to the conservatory
and Millicent approaches.
"I want you to know that you are one of
the reasons why I showed up."

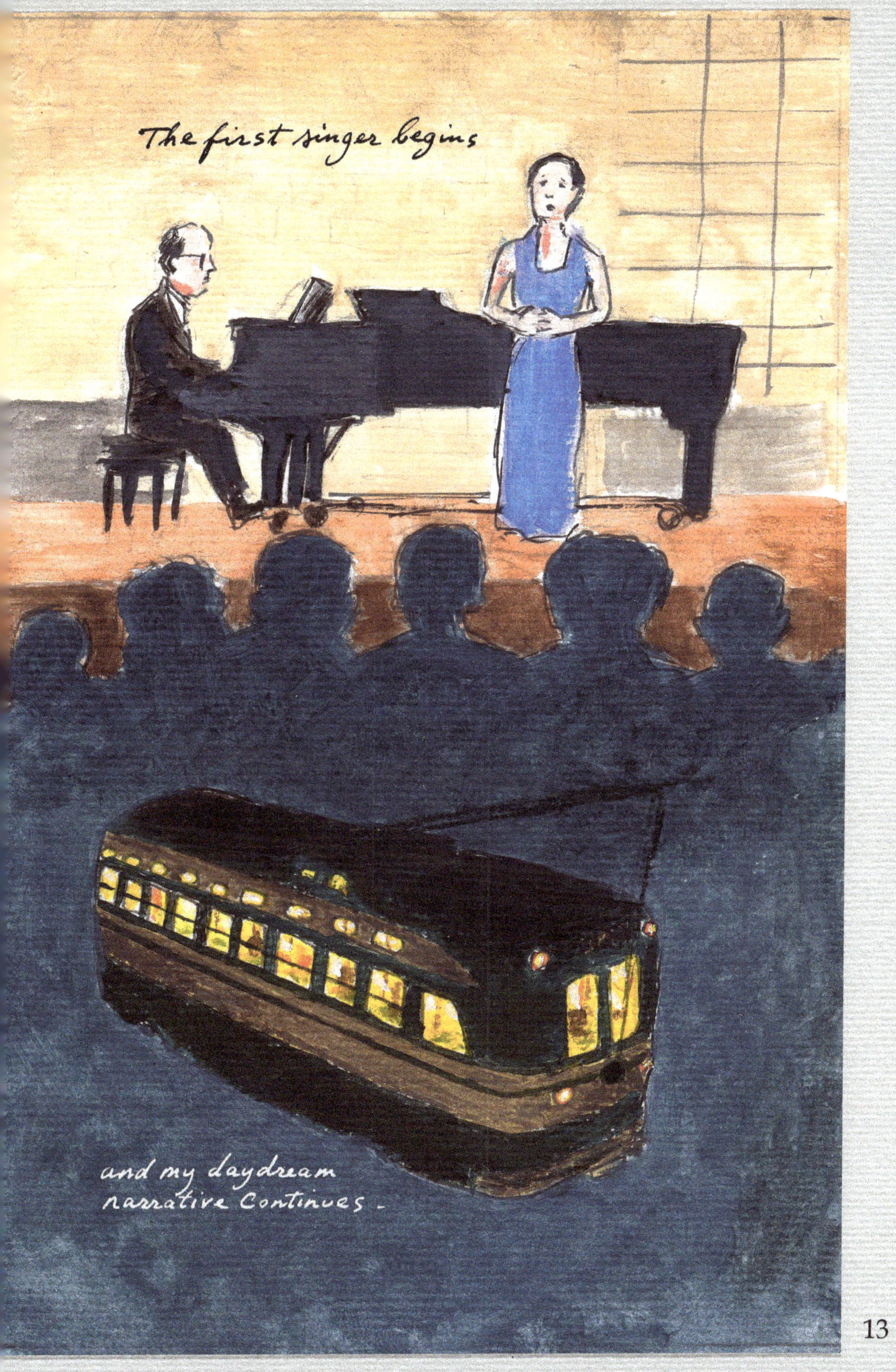

The first singer begins
and my daydream narrative continues -

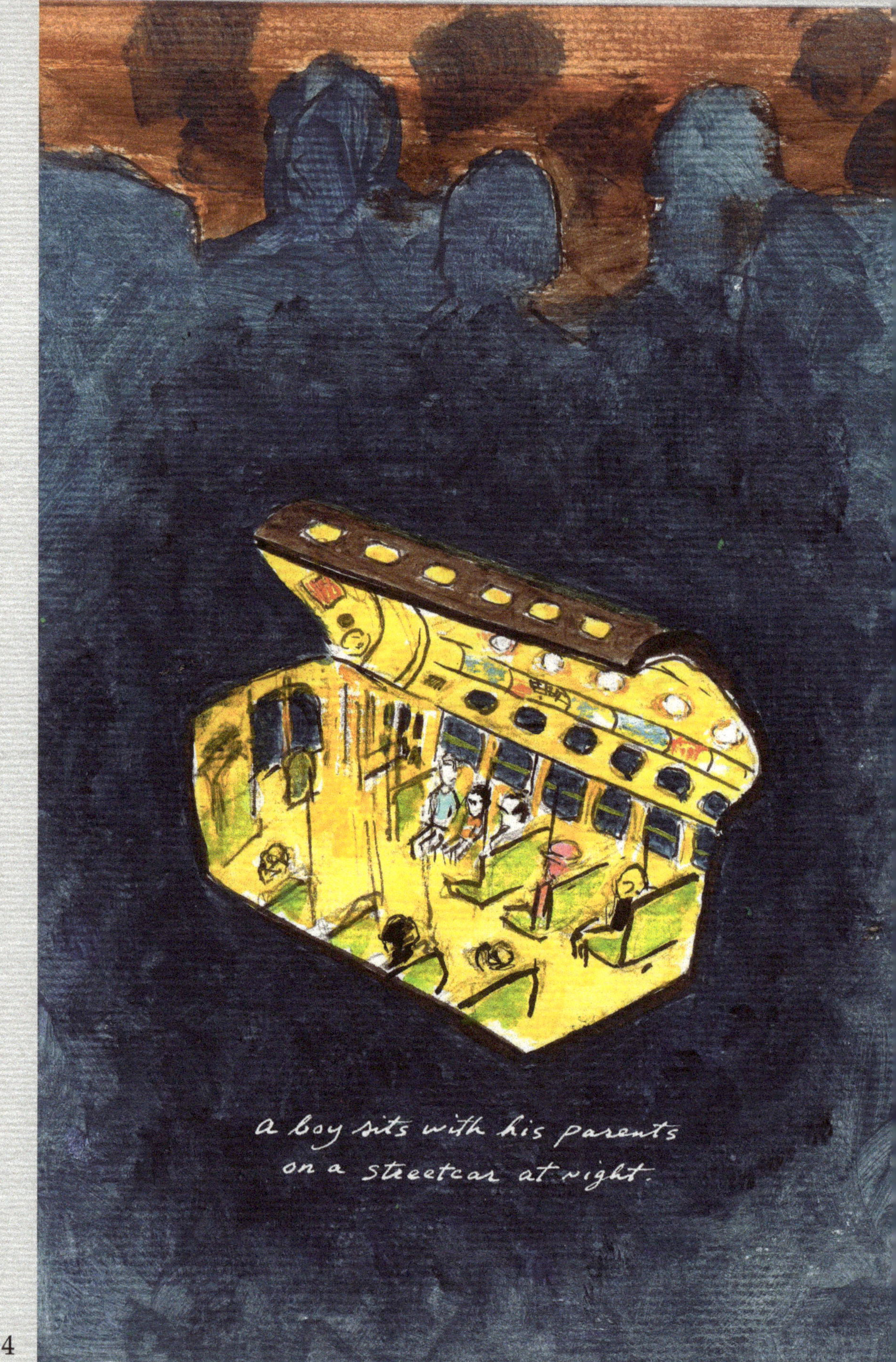

a boy sits with his parents
on a streetcar at night.

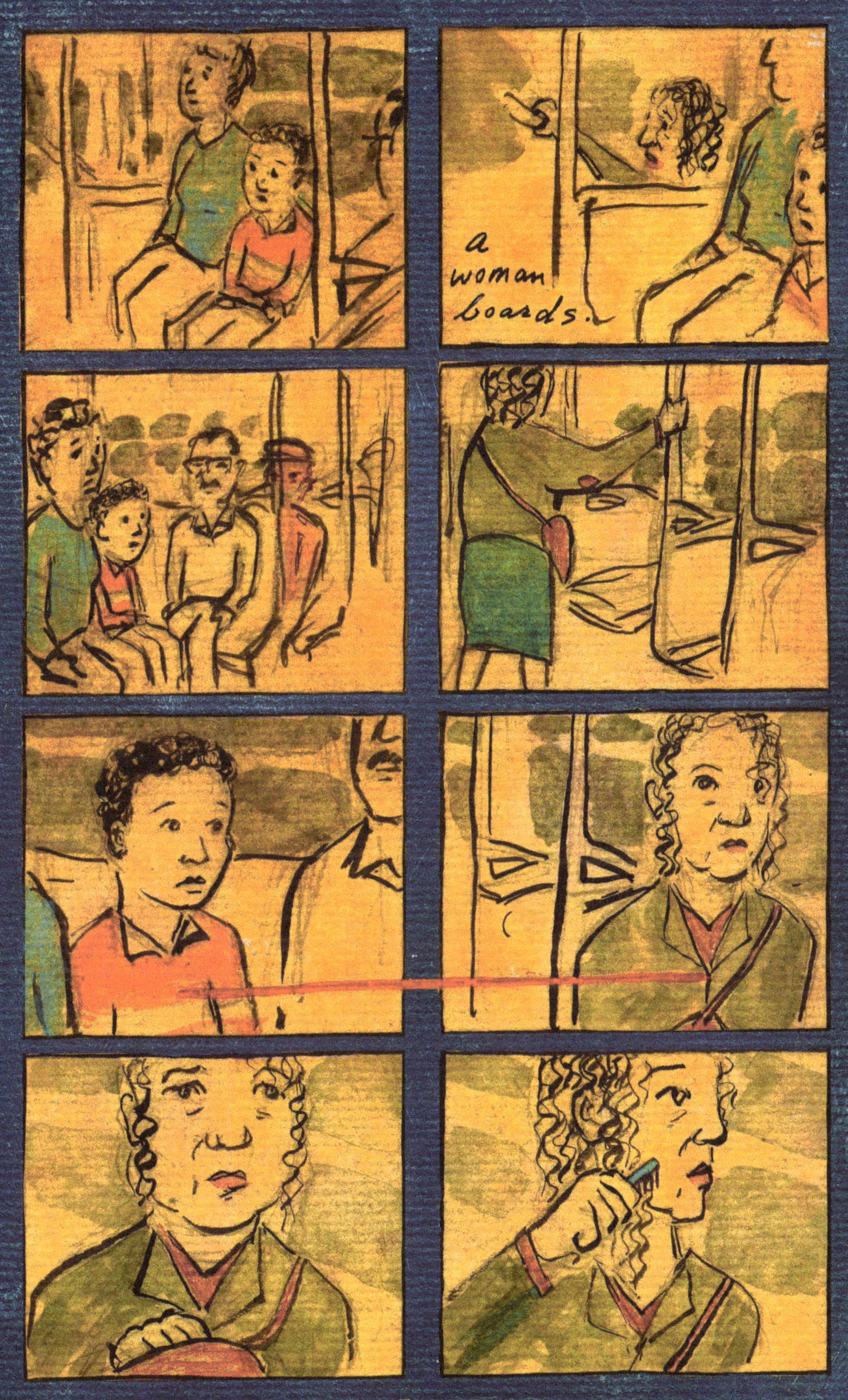
a
woman
boards.

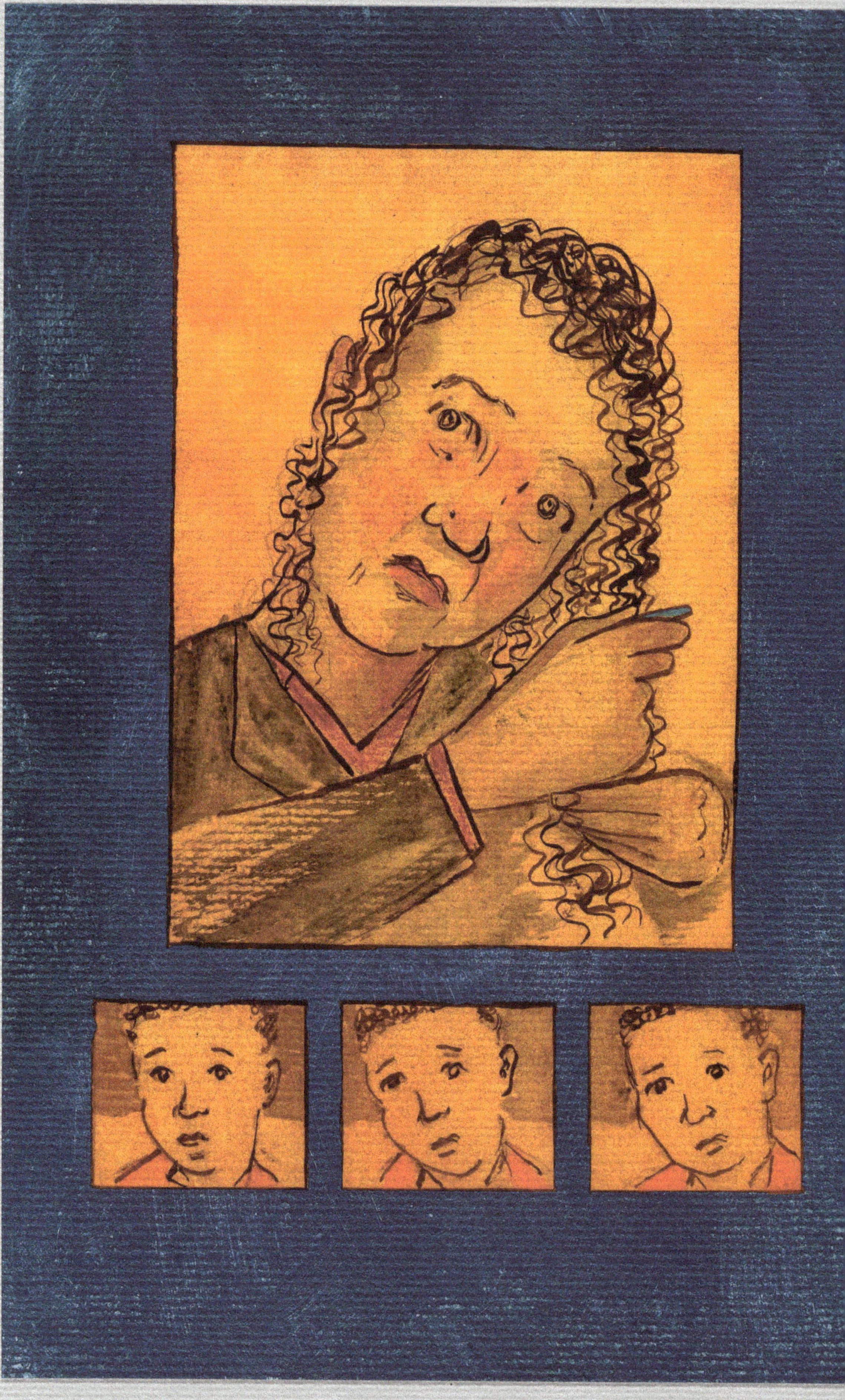

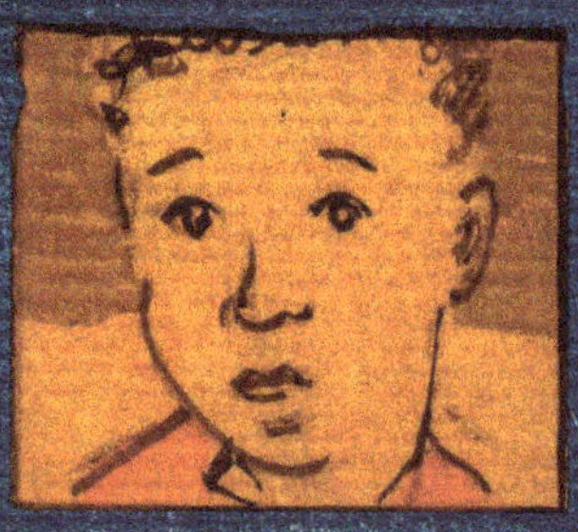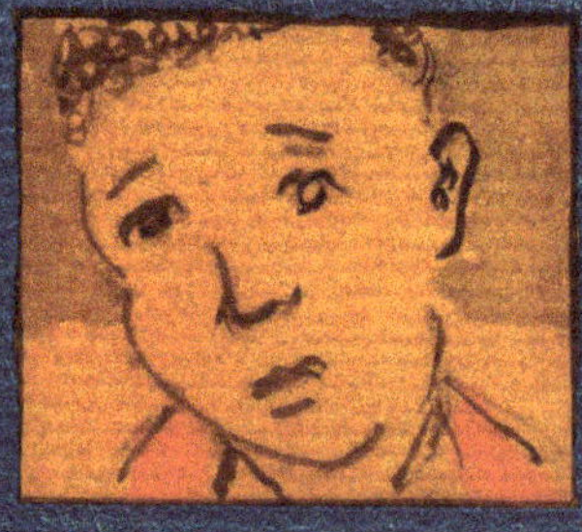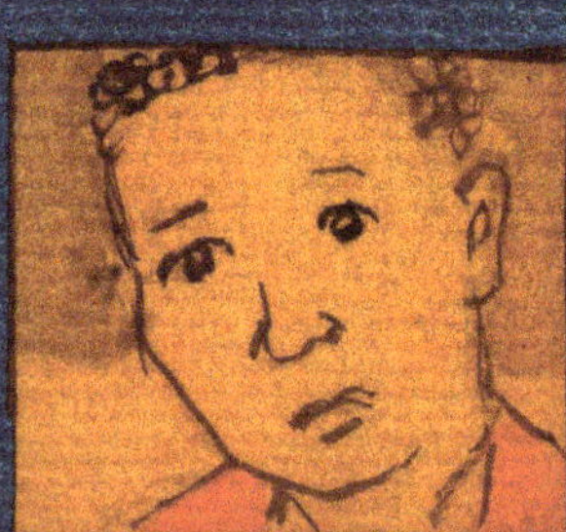

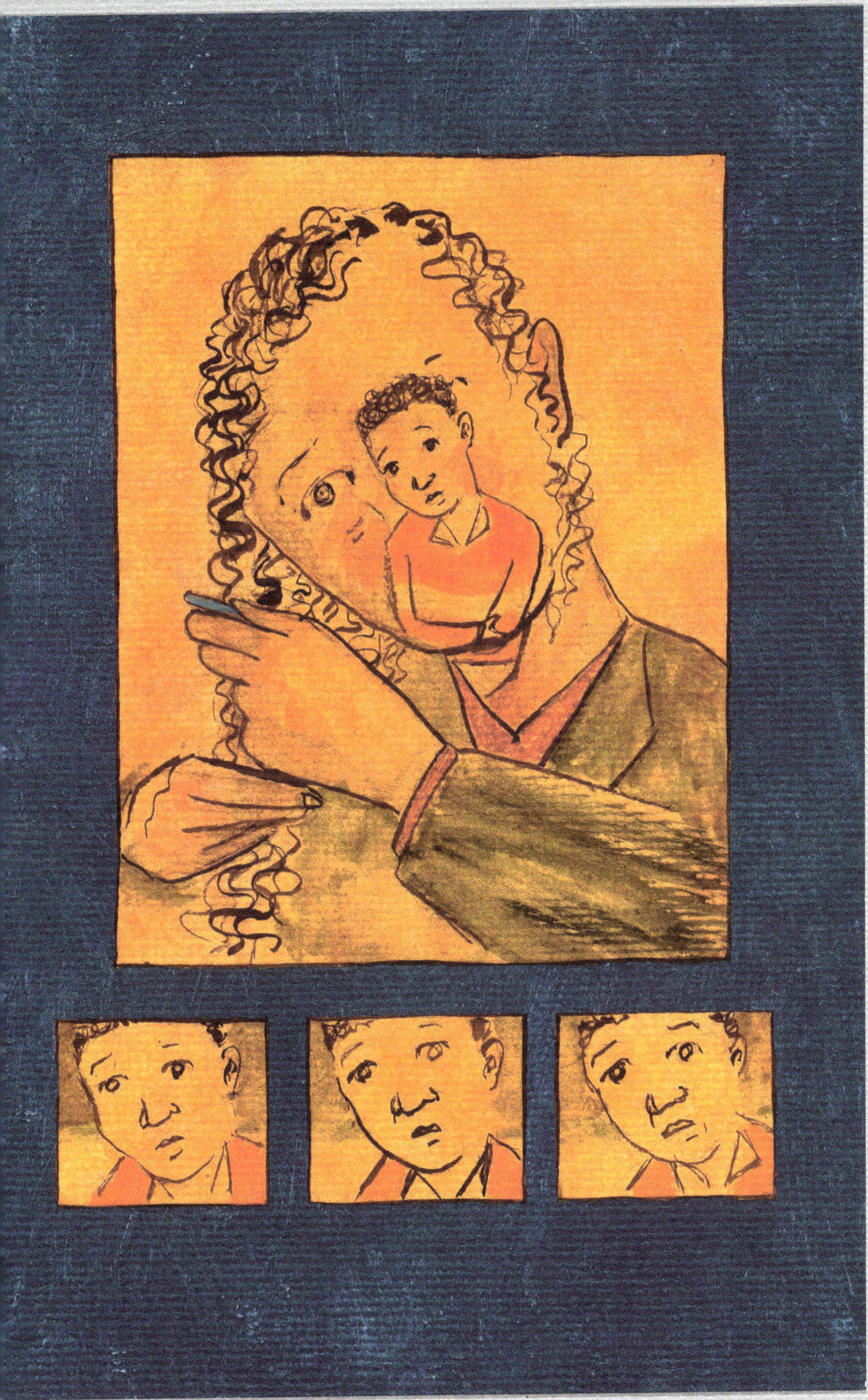

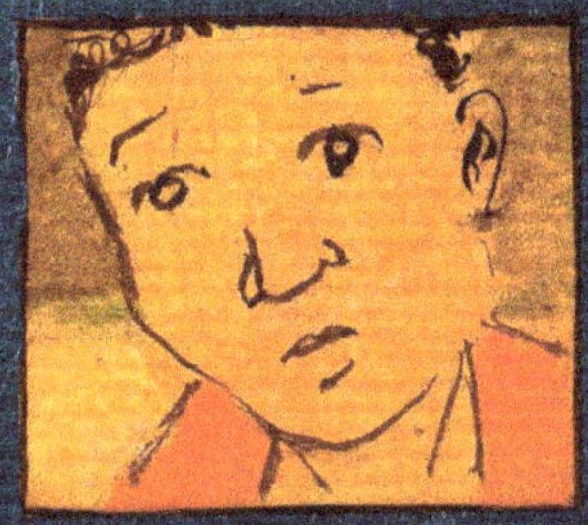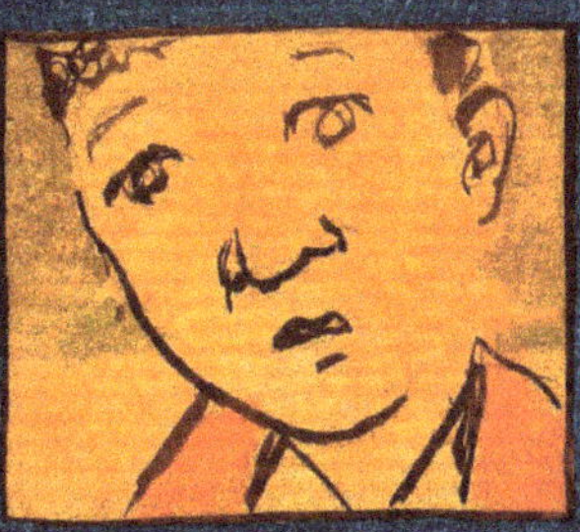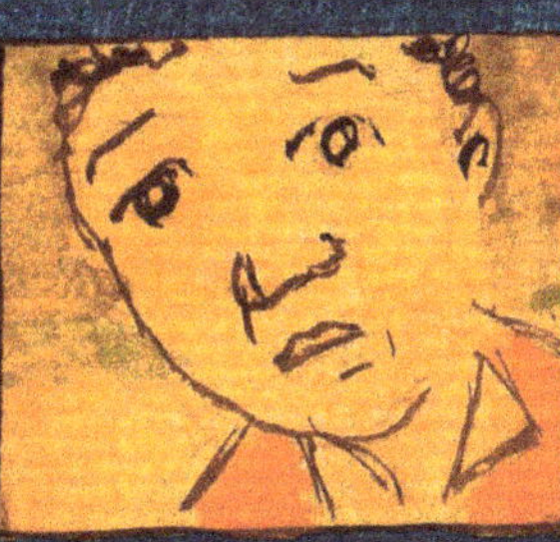

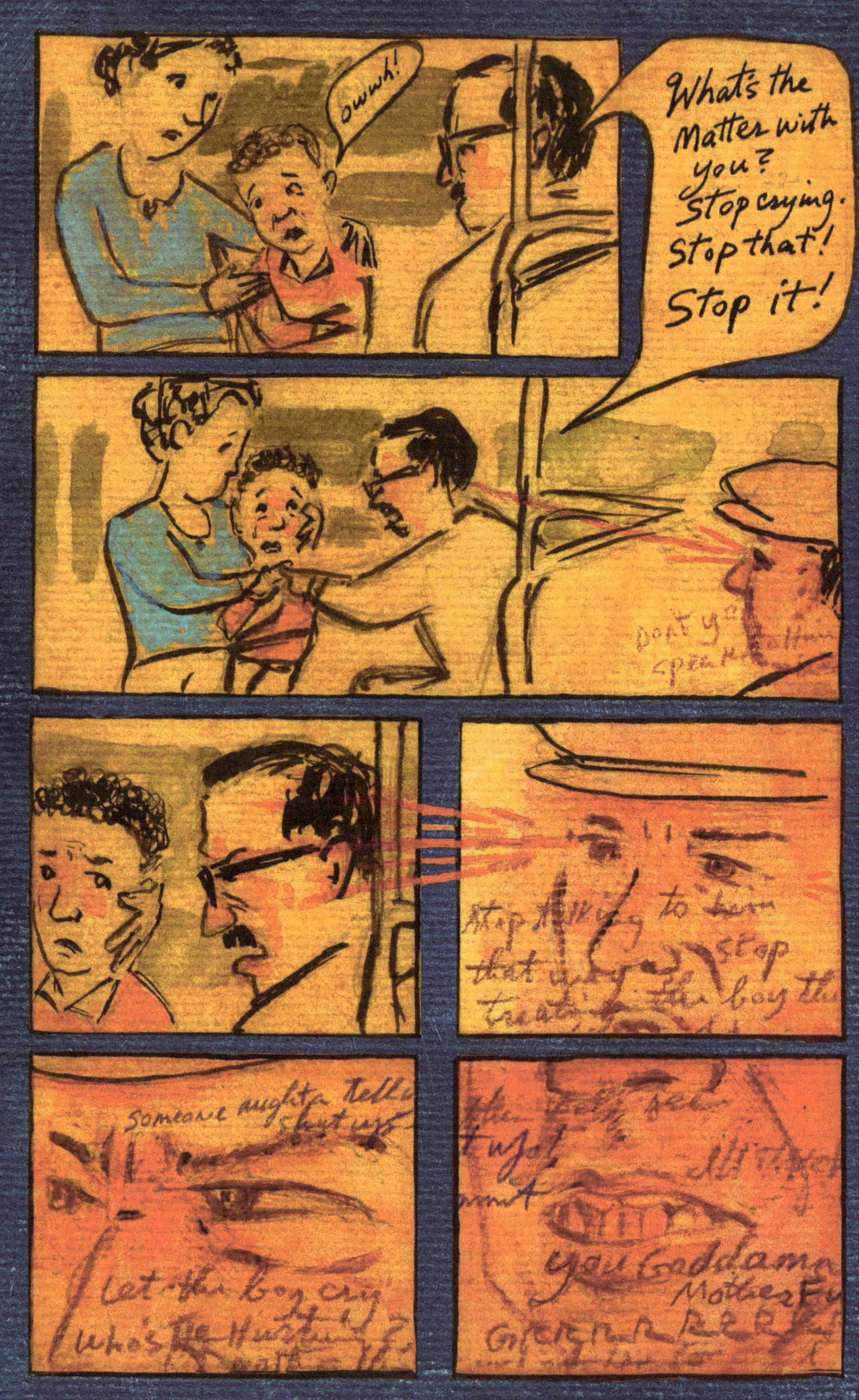

owwwh!
What's the matter with you? Stop crying. Stop that! Stop it!
Don't y'a speak to me
stop trying to burn that lady stop treating the boy th
someone aughta tell shut up
Let the boy cry who's he hurting
you Goddamn mother fu

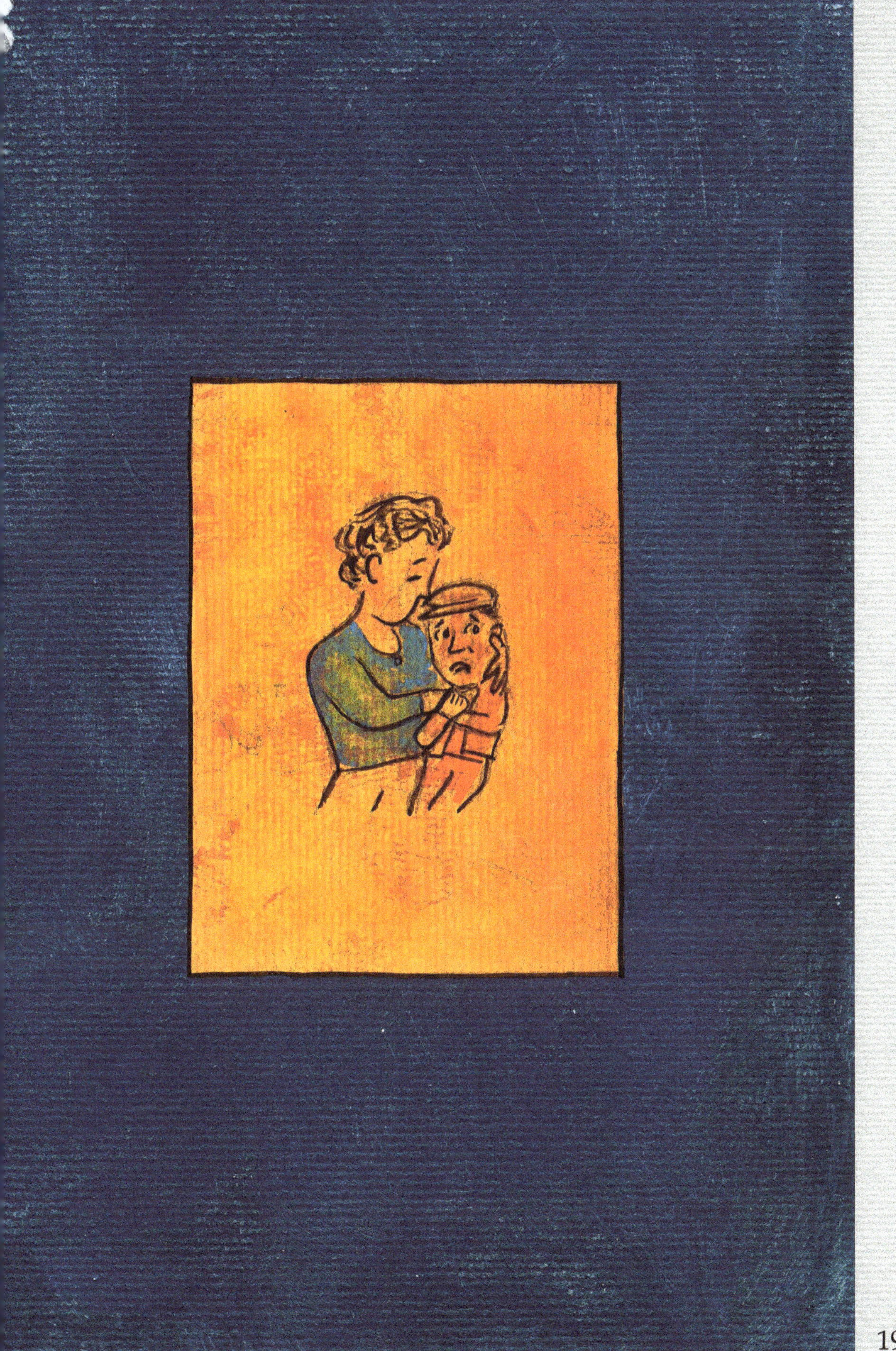

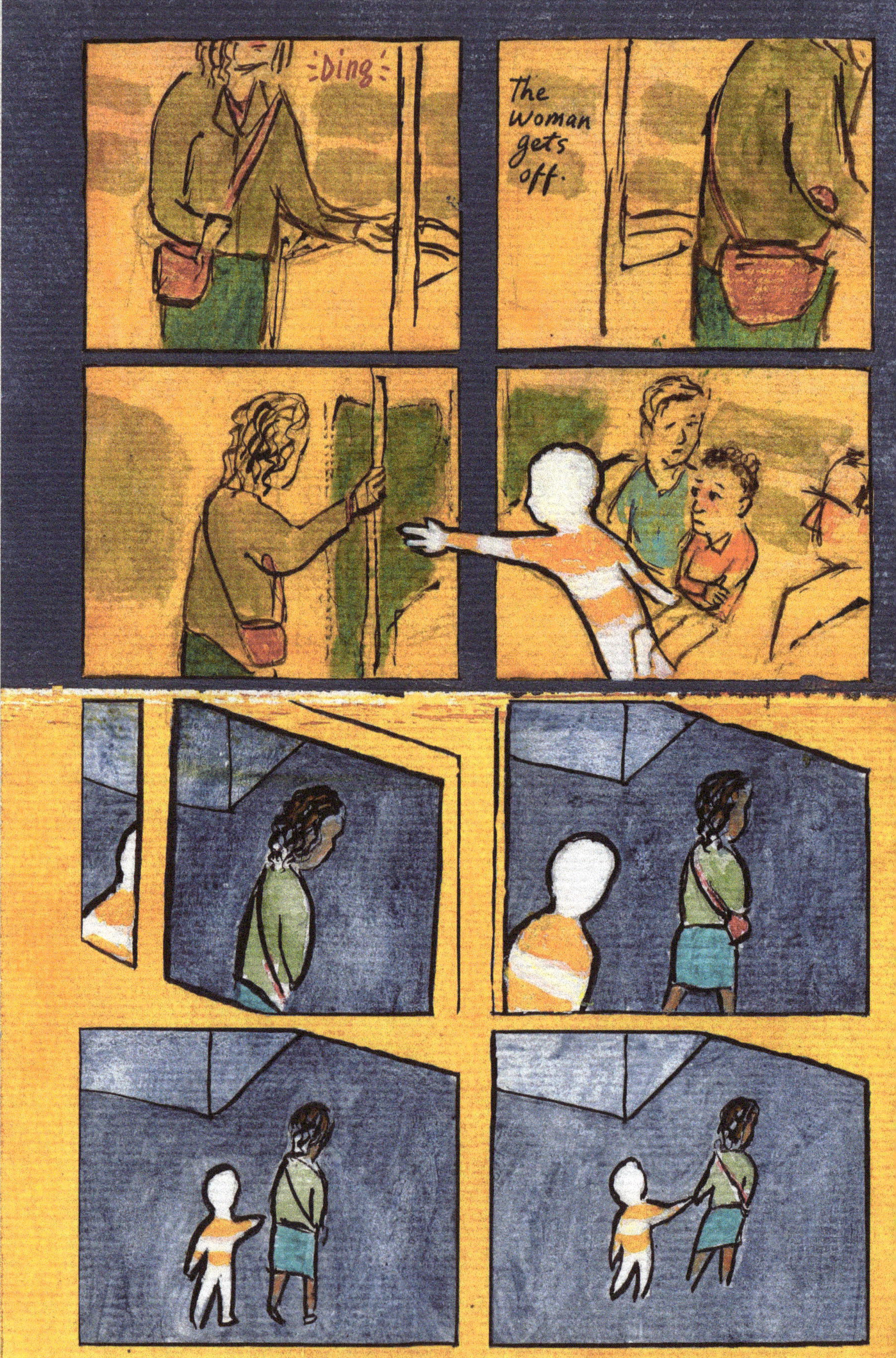
Ding
The Woman gets off.

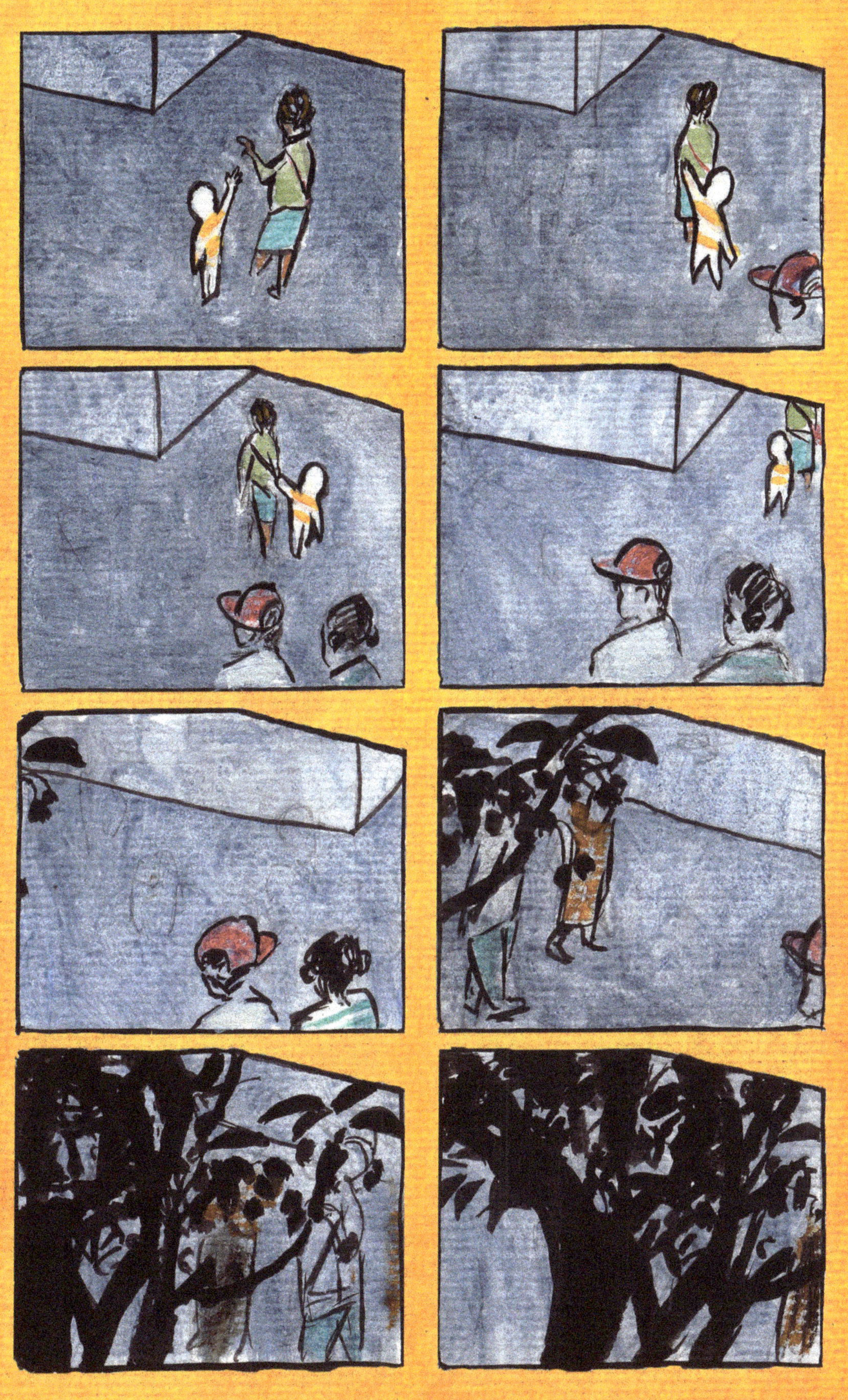

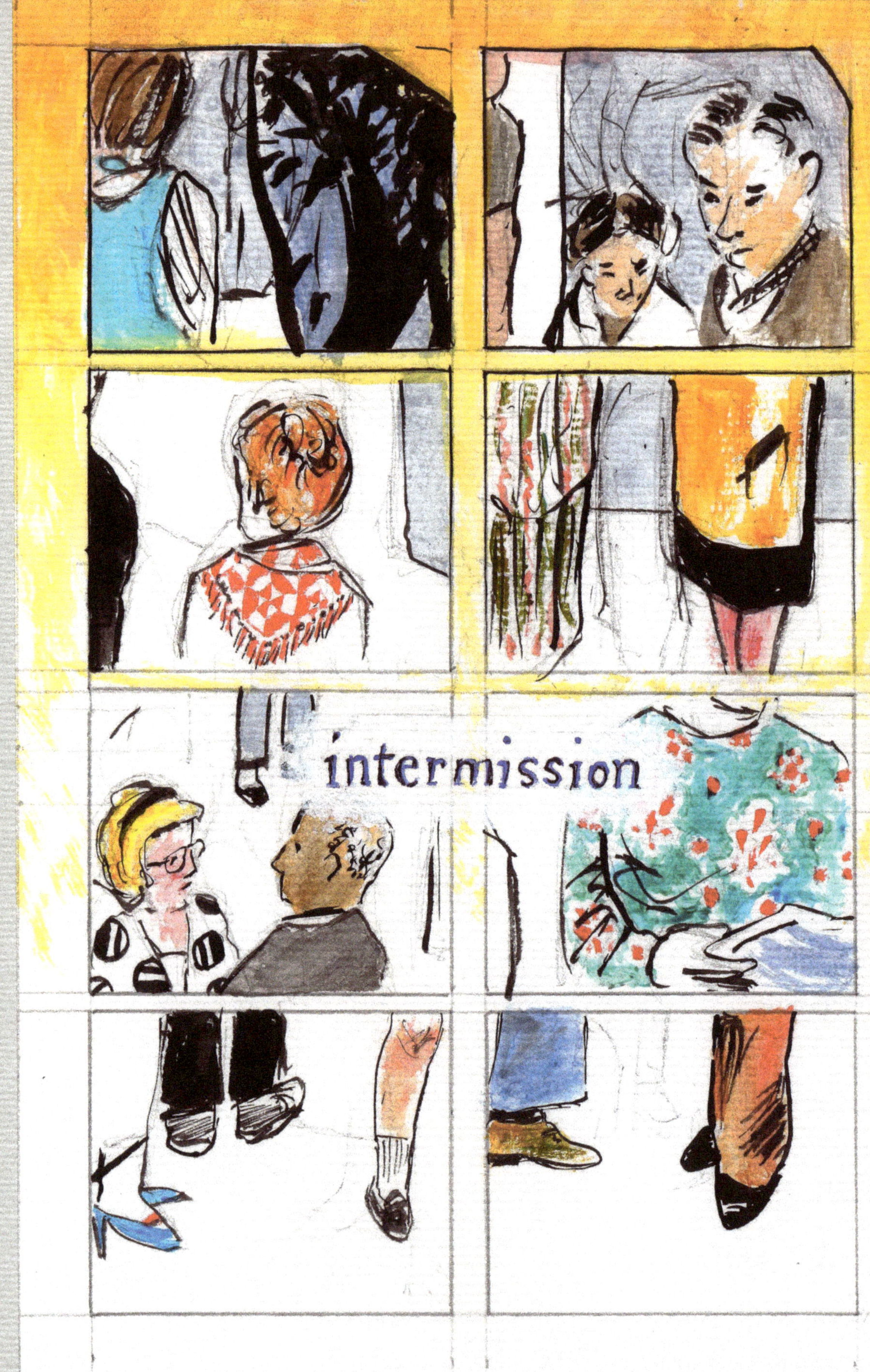
intermission

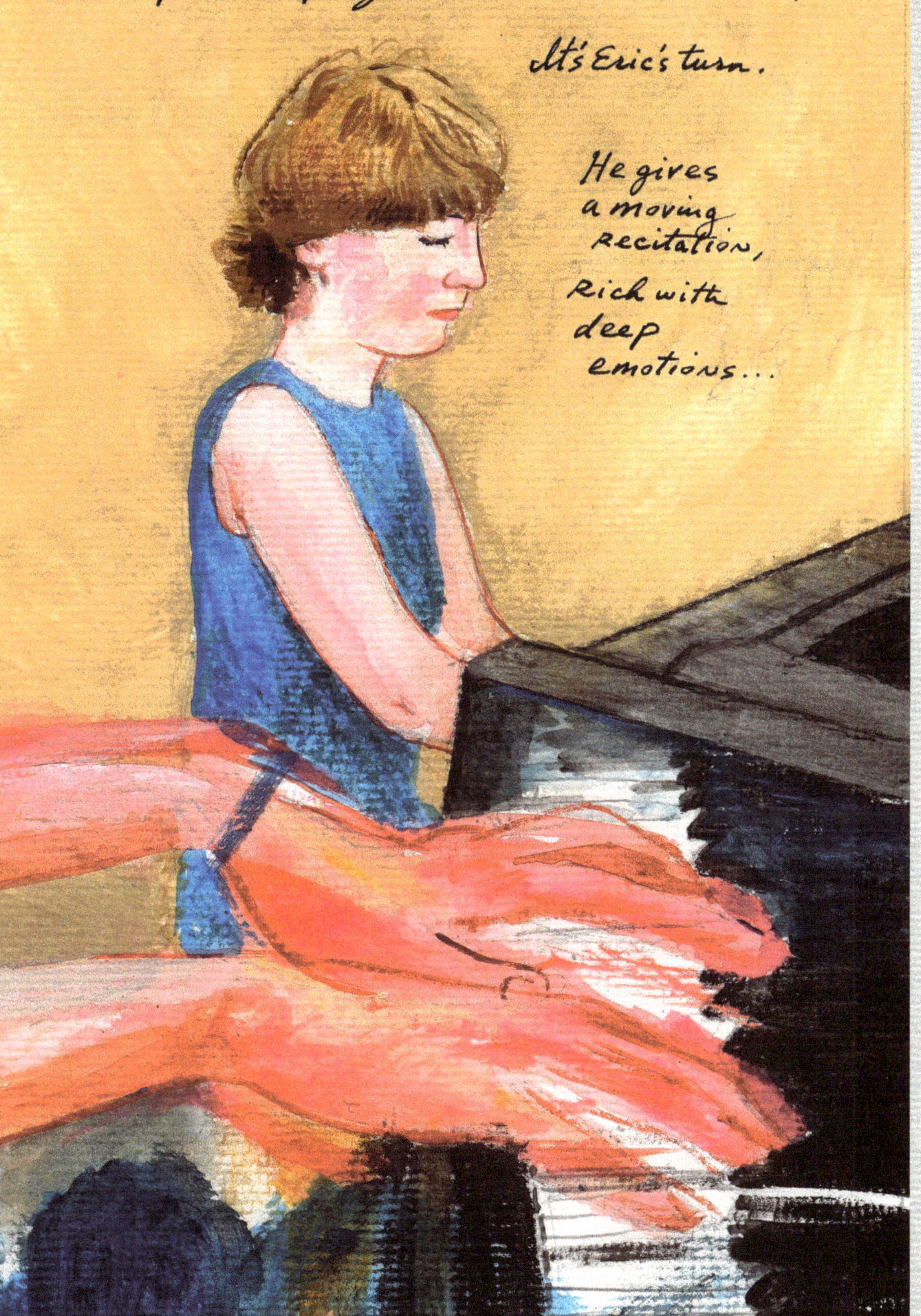

I return to the concert hall with the others.
The pianist plays the intro.

It's Eric's turn.

He gives
a moving
recitation,
Rich with
deep
emotions...

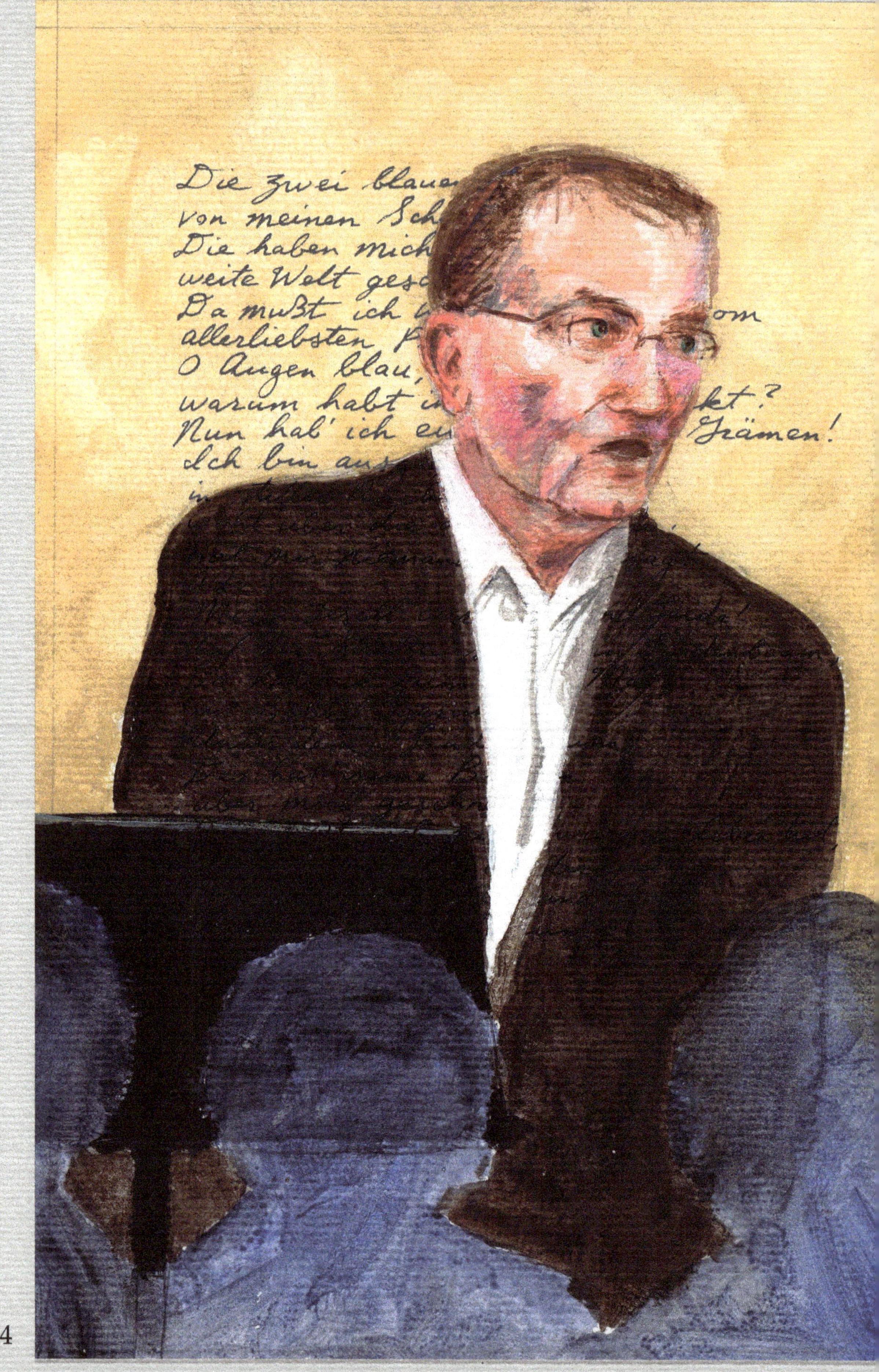

Die zwei blauen
von meinen Sch
Die haben mich
weite Welt gesch
Da mußt ich
allerliebsten
O Augen blau,
warum habt i   kt?
Nun hab' ich eu   Grämen!
Ich bin au

The two blue eyes
of my darling
they sent me into
the wide world.
I had to take my leave of this
most-beloved place!
O blue eyes,
why do you gaze on me?
Now I have eternal sorrow
and grief.
I went out into the quiet night
well across the dark heath.
To me no one bade farewell.
Farewell!
My companions are love and
    sorrow!
By the road stood a linden tree,
    Where, for the first time,
I found rest in sleep!
Under the linden tree
that snowed its blossoms
over me,
I did not know how life went on,
and all was well again!
All! All, love and sorrow
and world and dream!

25

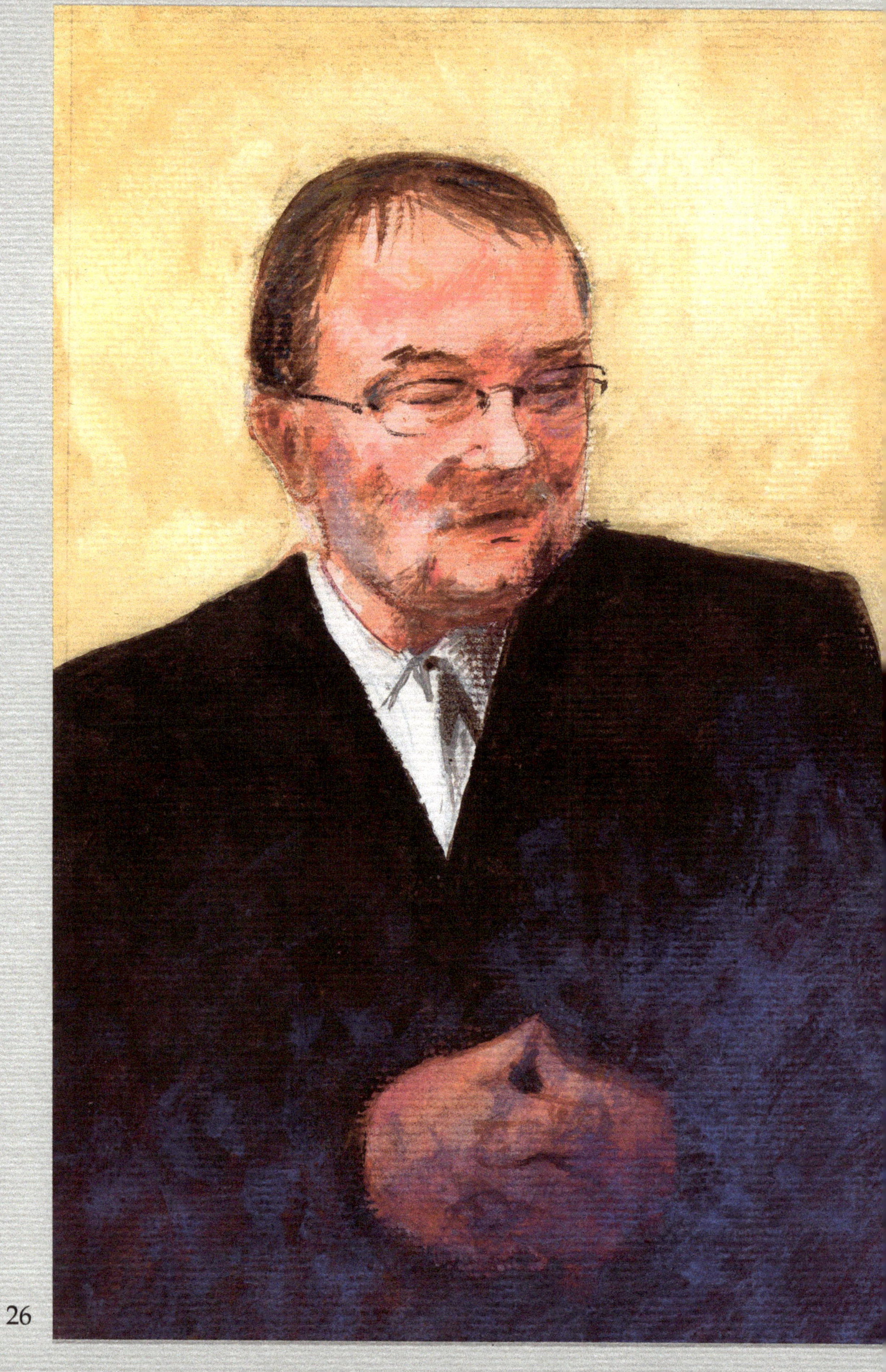

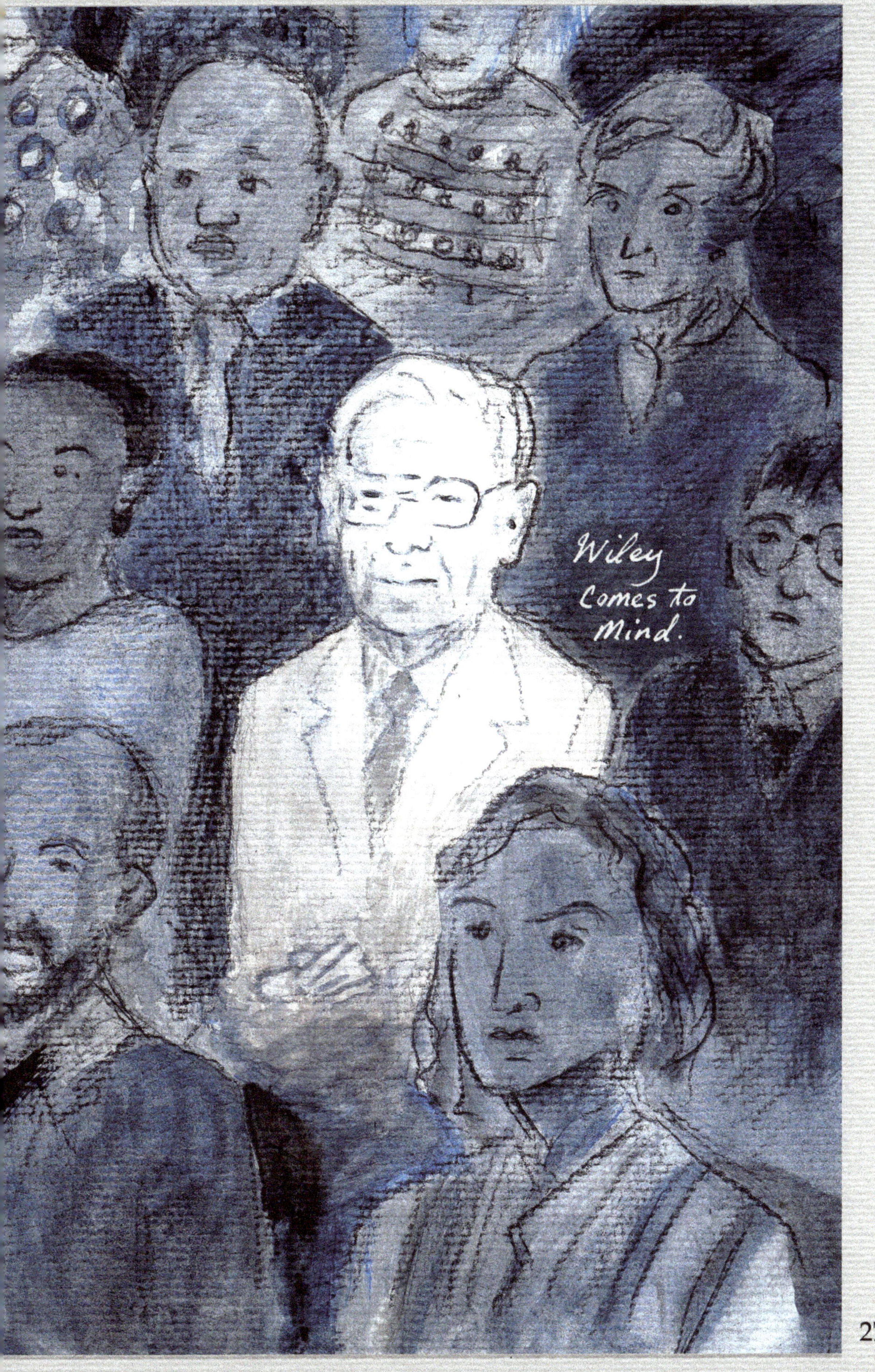

Wiley comes to mind.

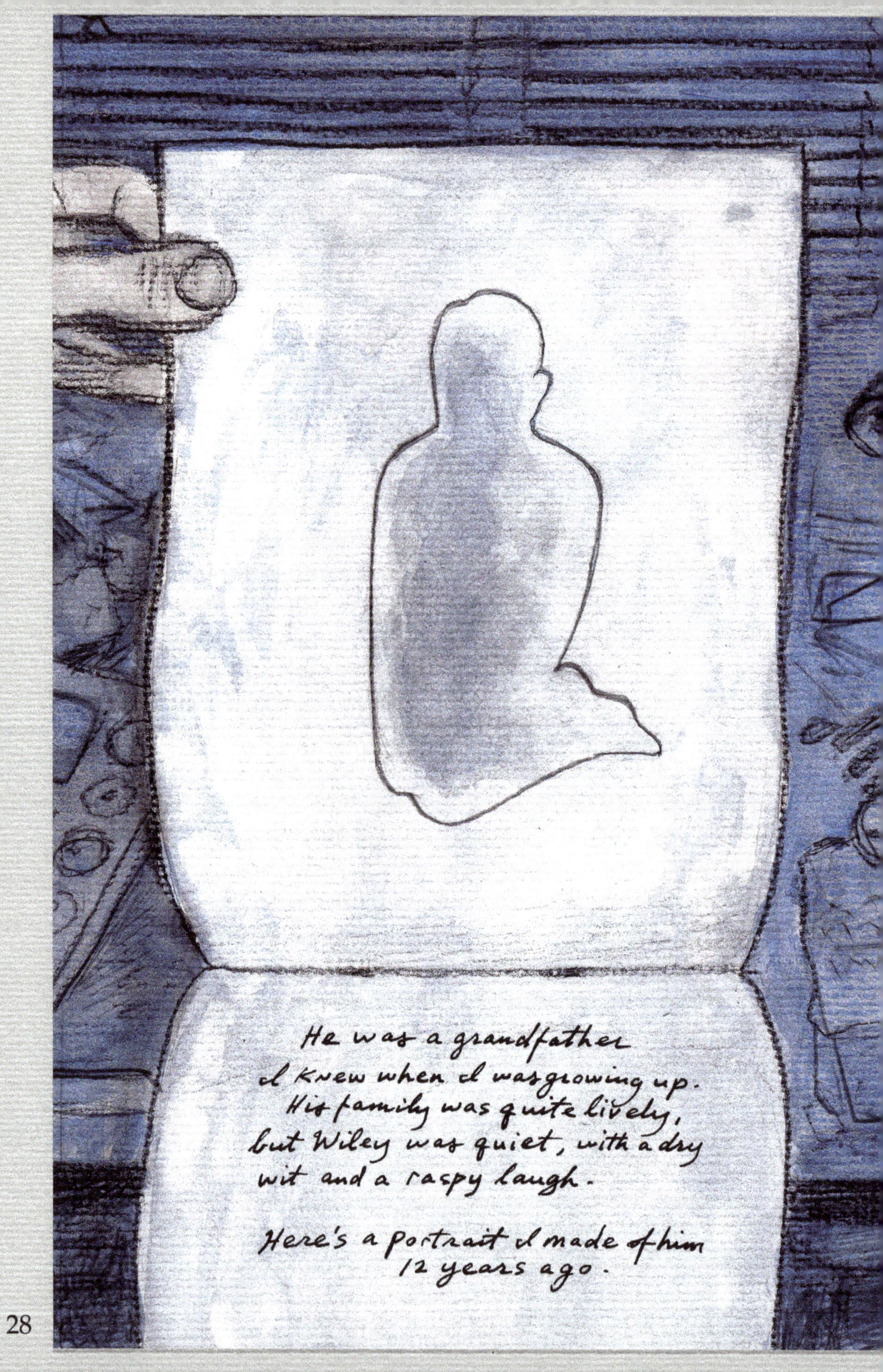

He was a grandfather
I knew when I was growing up.
His family was quite lively,
but Wiley was quiet, with a dry
wit and a raspy laugh.

Here's a portrait I made of him
12 years ago.

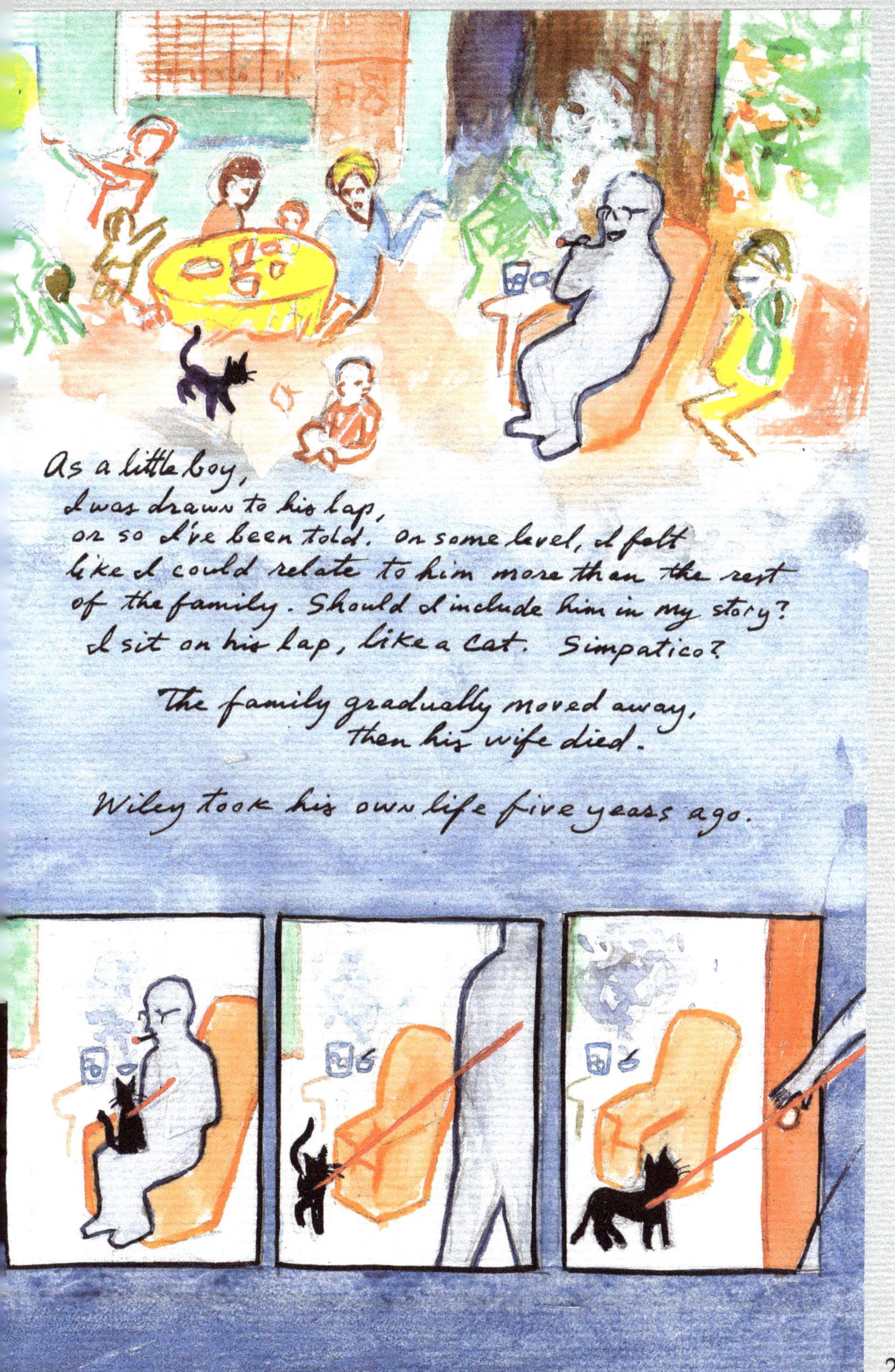

As a little boy,
I was drawn to his lap,
or so I've been told. On some level, I felt
like I could relate to him more than the rest
of the family. Should I include him in my story?
I sit on his lap, like a cat. Simpatico?

The family gradually moved away,
then his wife died.

Wiley took his own life five years ago.

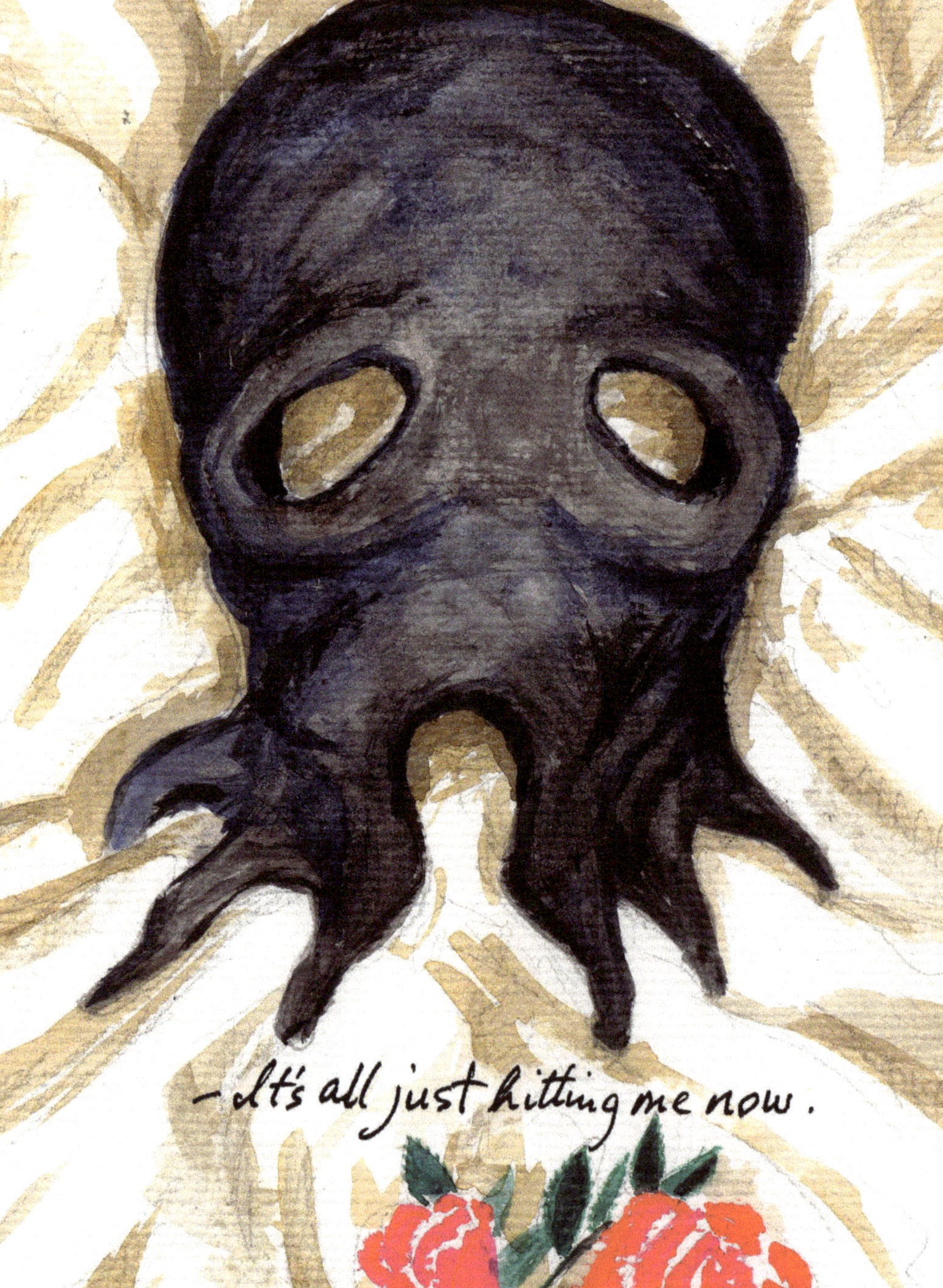

Dare I include a shot of him from the wake?
our connection...
his death from despair...
– It's all just hitting me now.

A bass on stage interrupts the memory.
He sings with great gusto
a declaration from the Messiah:

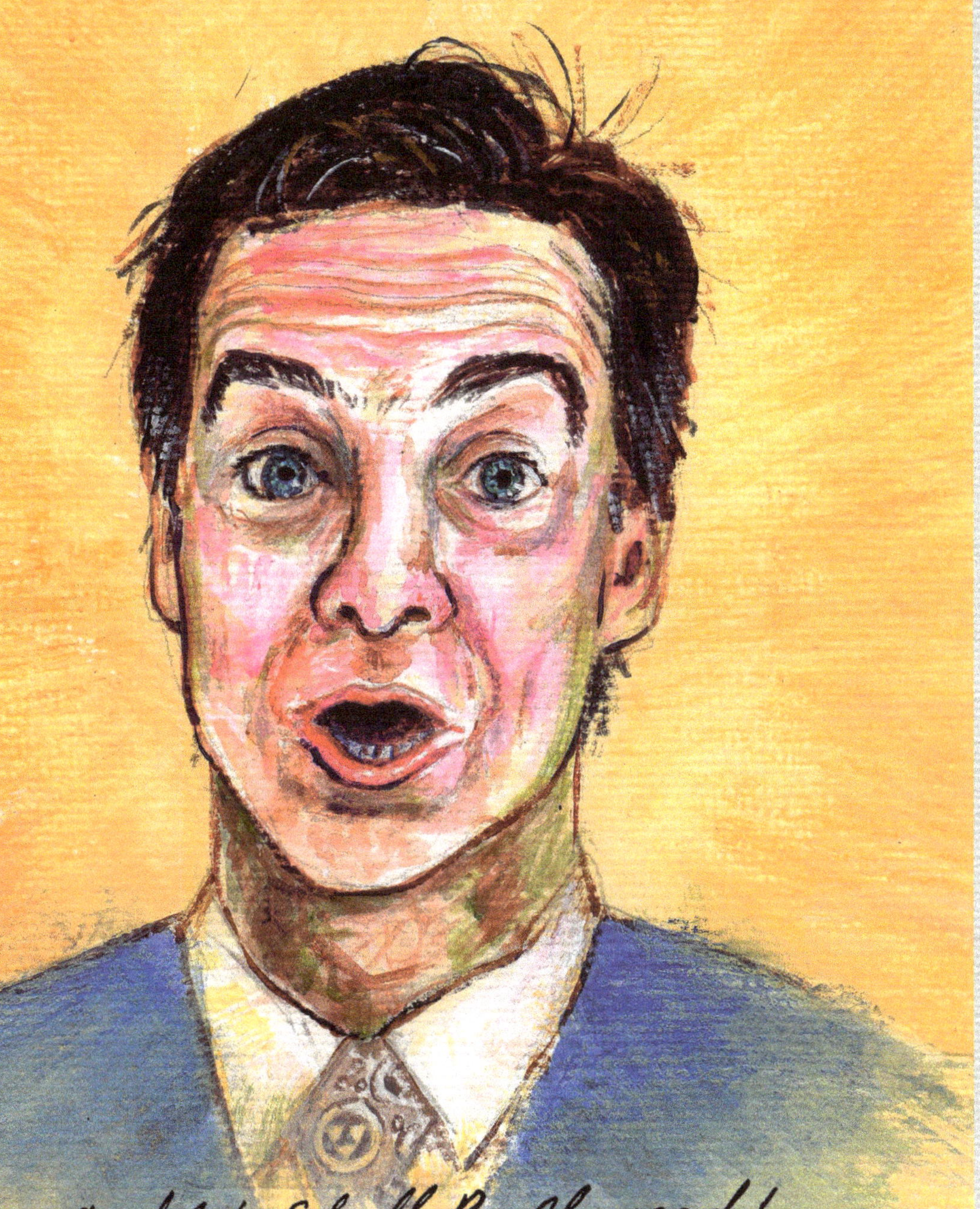

And We Shall Be Changed!
And We Shall Be Changed!
And We Shall Be Changed!

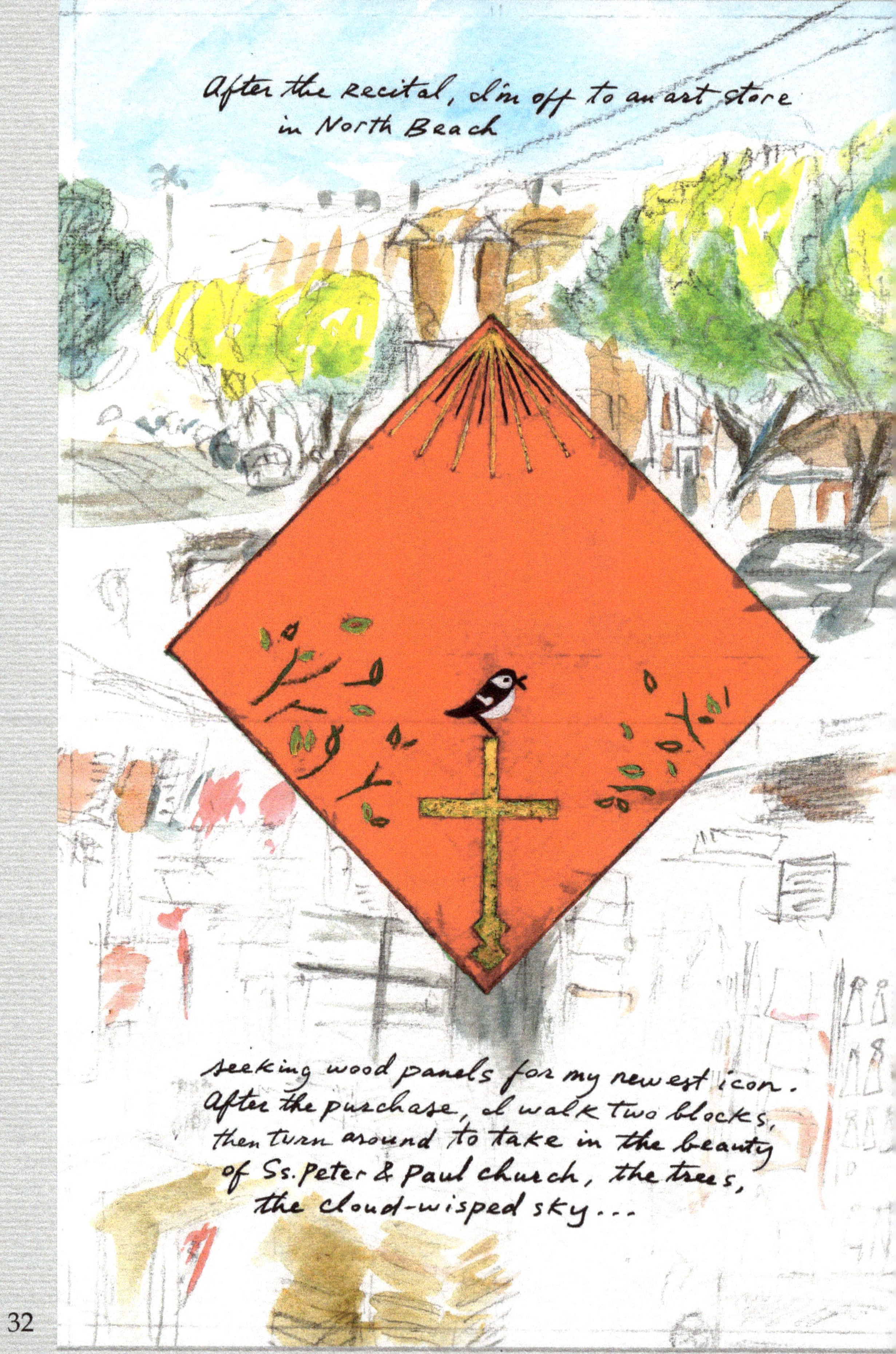

After the recital, I'm off to an art store
in North Beach

seeking wood panels for my newest icon.
After the purchase, I walk two blocks,
then turn around to take in the beauty
of Ss. Peter & Paul church, the trees,
the cloud-wisped sky...

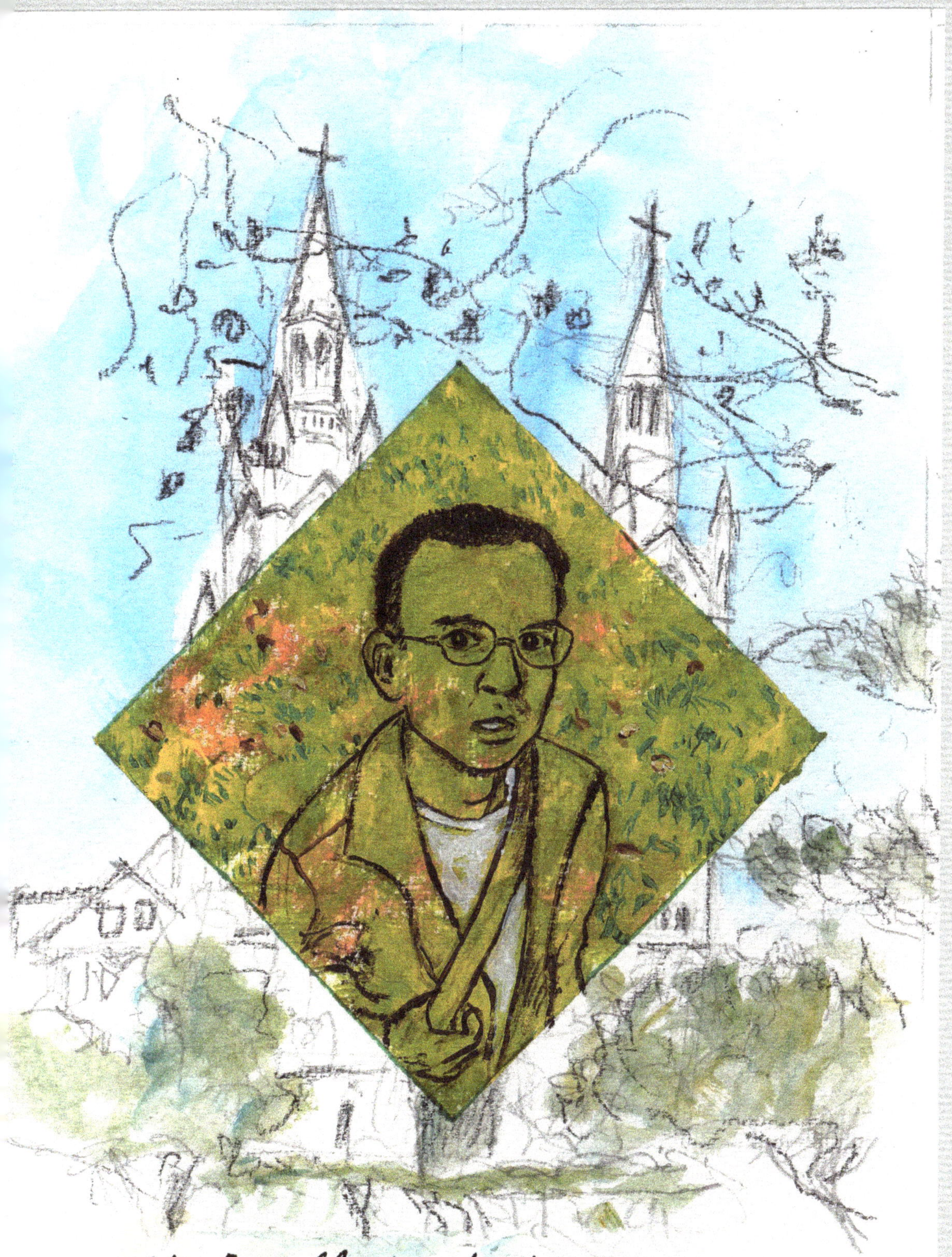

Aha! A black and white bird is perched atop the gold cross on the church, just like in my icon!
Seconds go by, and...

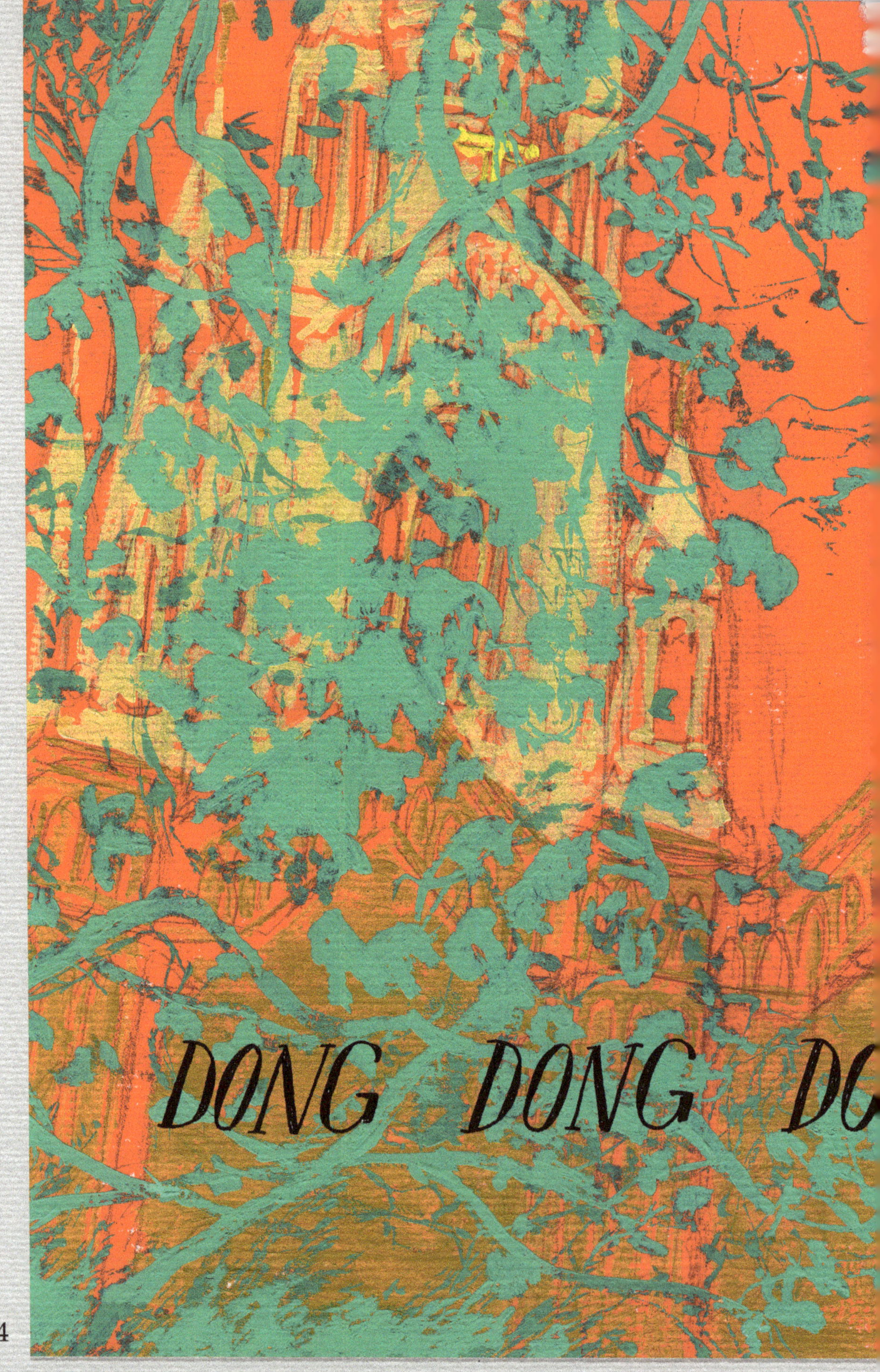

DONG DONG DO

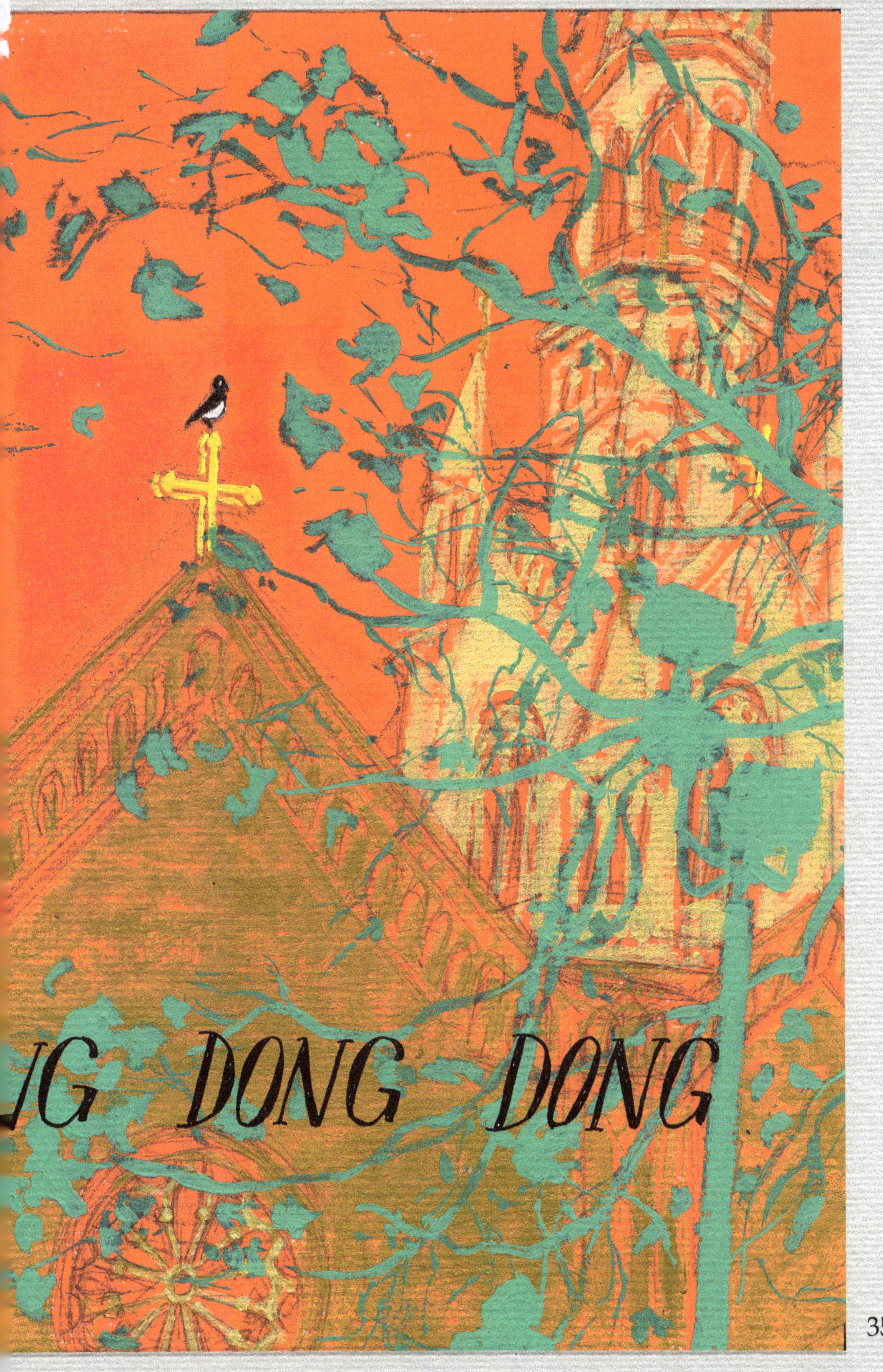

IG DONG DONG

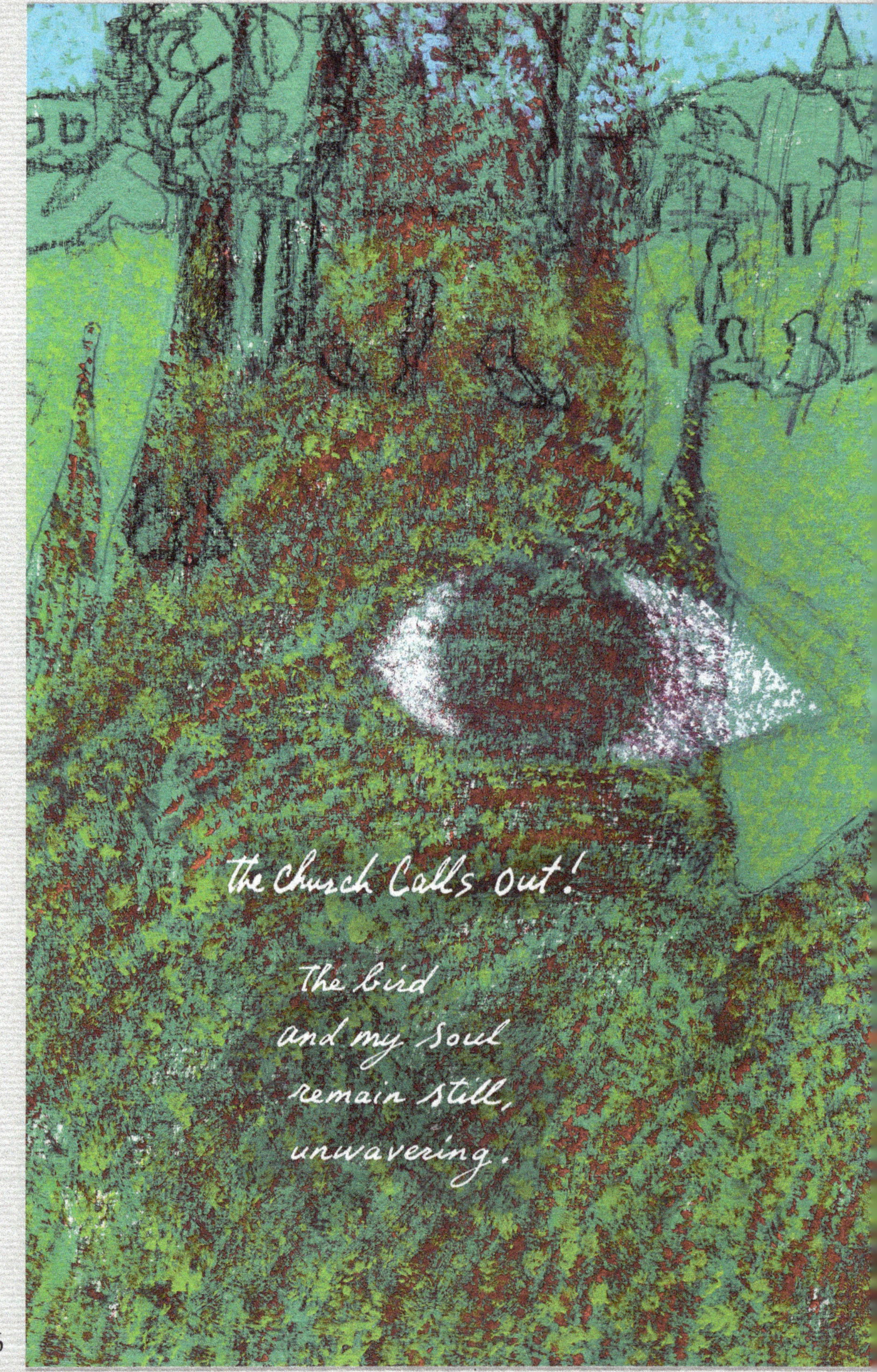

the church Calls out!

The bird
and my soul
remain still,
unwavering.

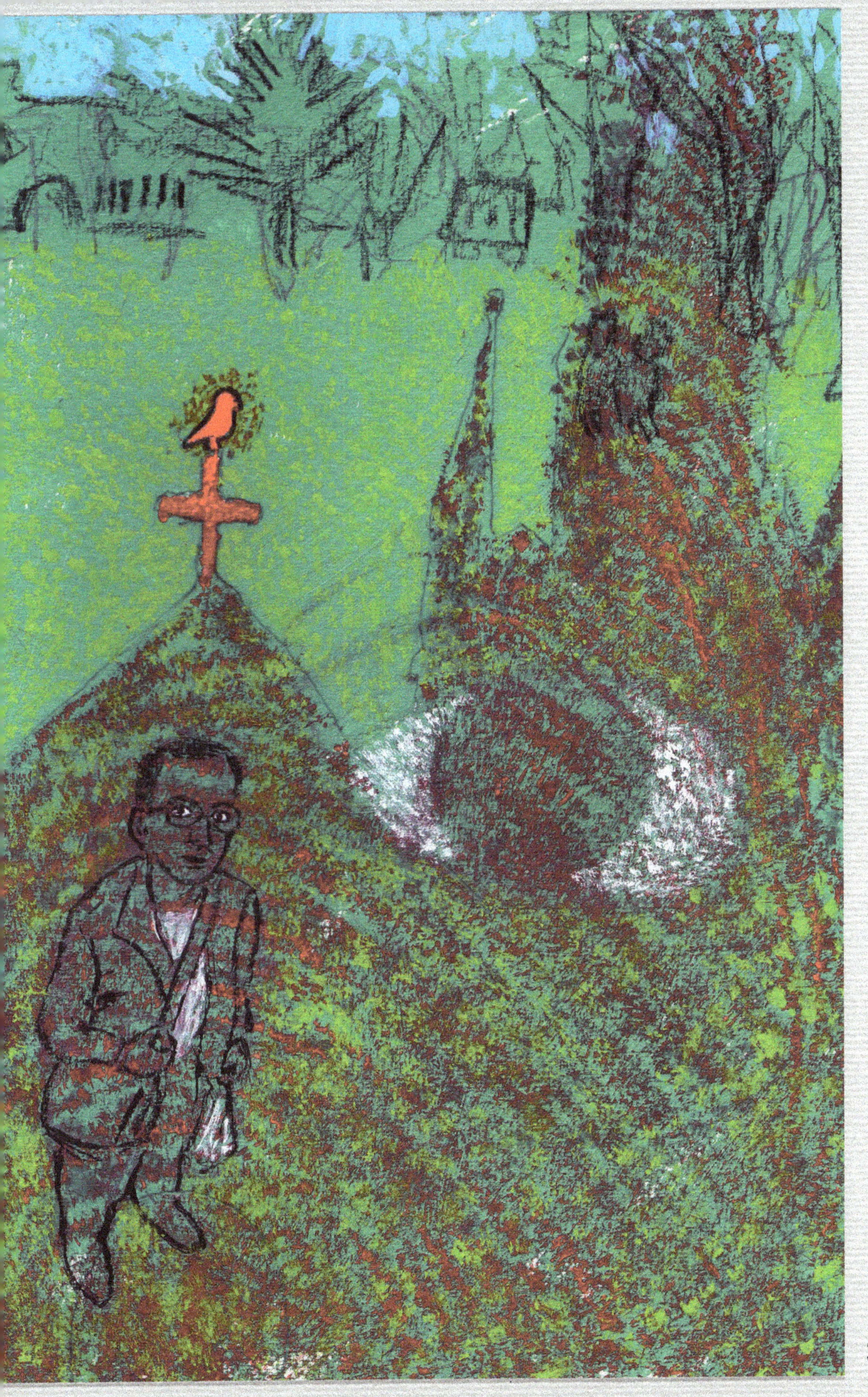

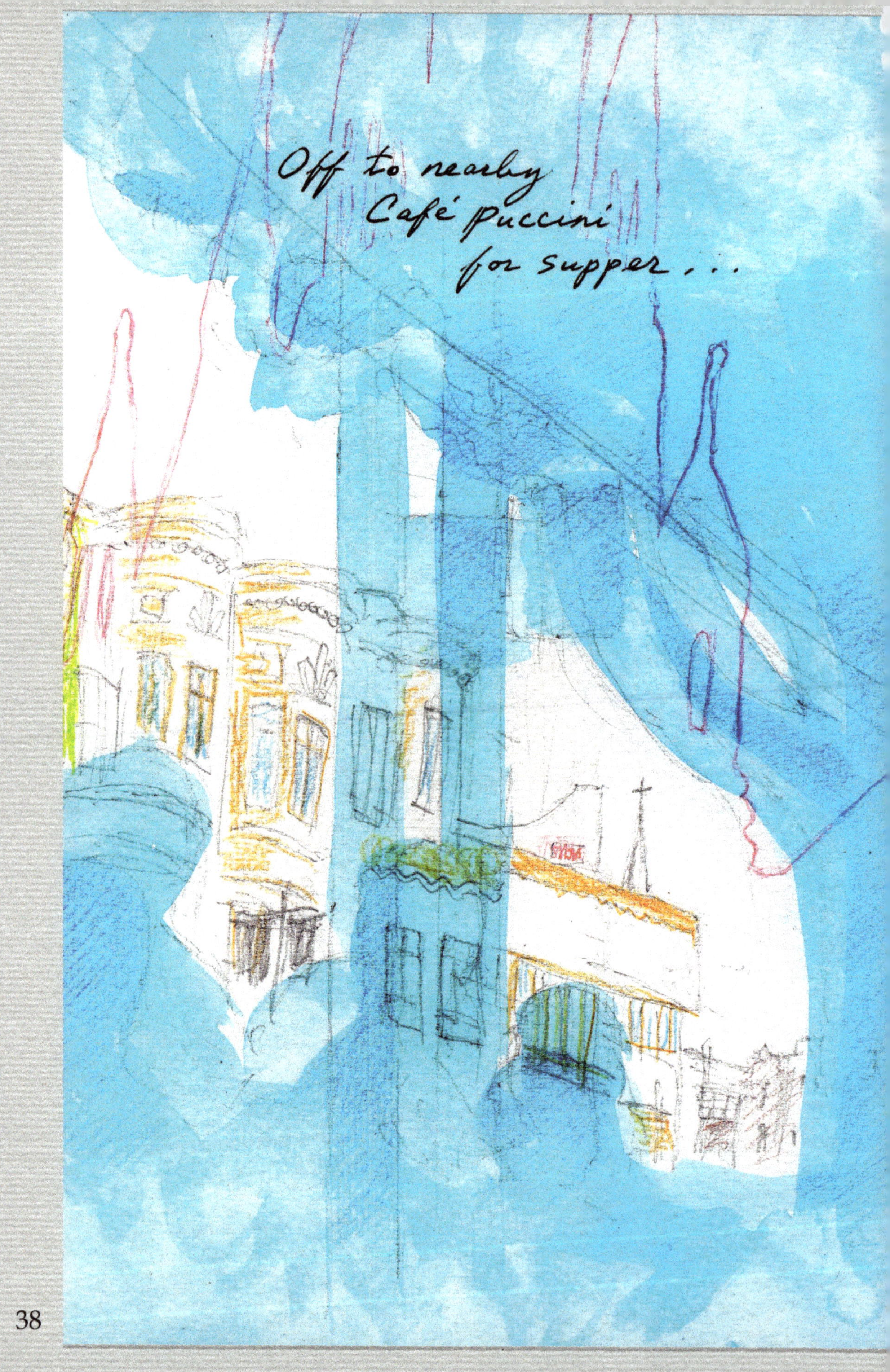
Off to nearby
Café Puccini
for supper . . .

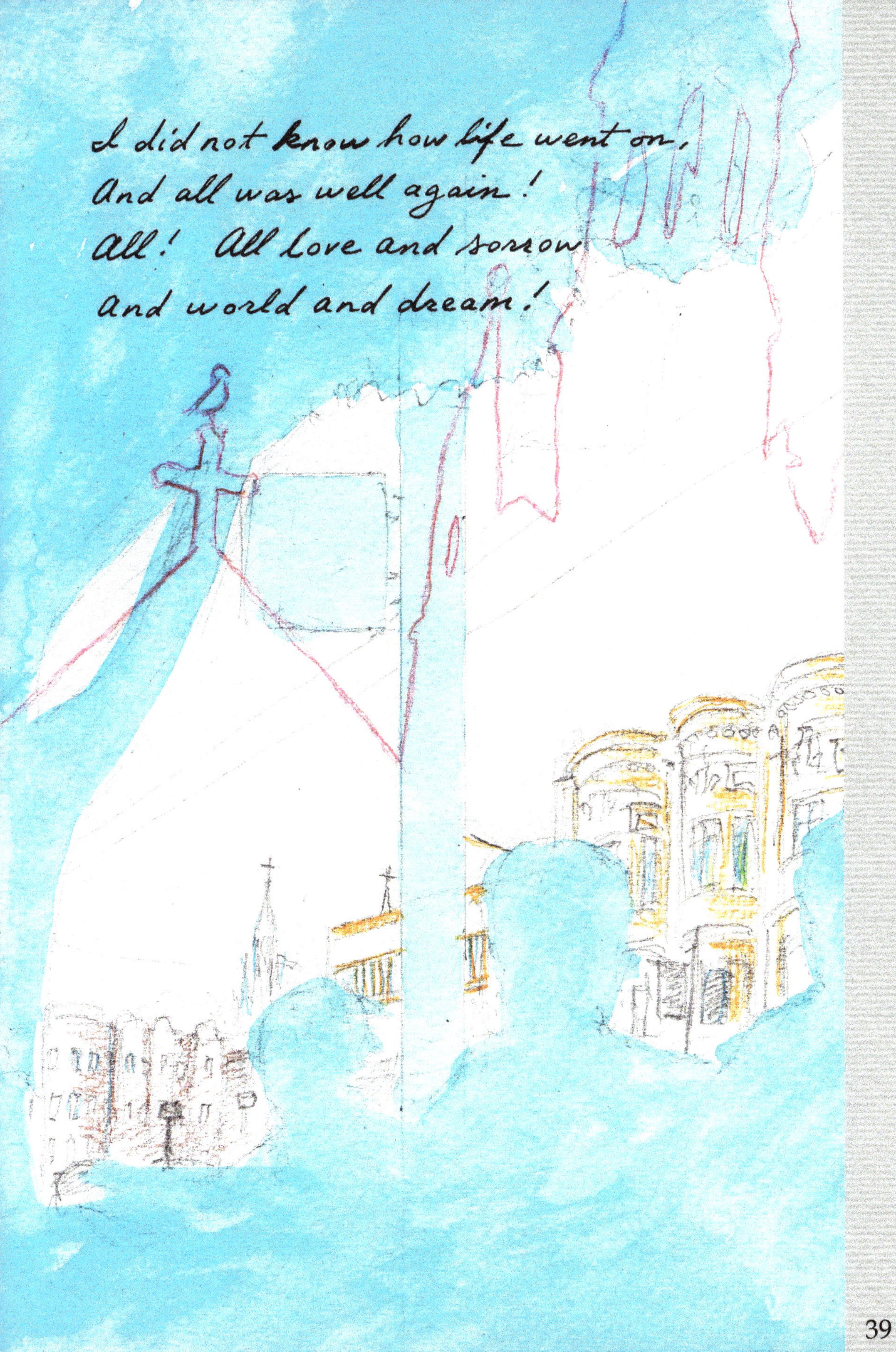
I did not know how life went on,
And all was well again!
All! All love and sorrow
And world and dream!

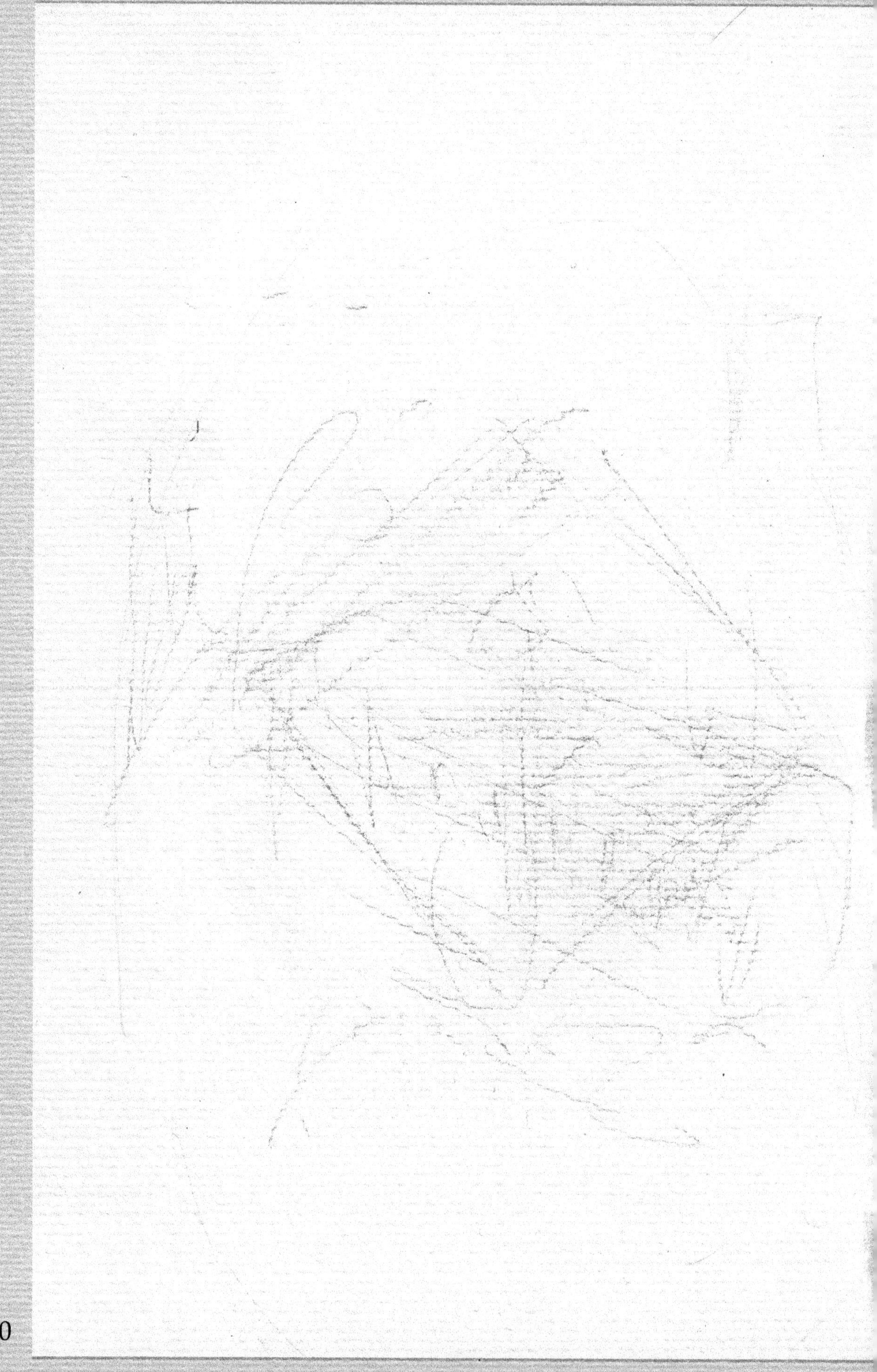

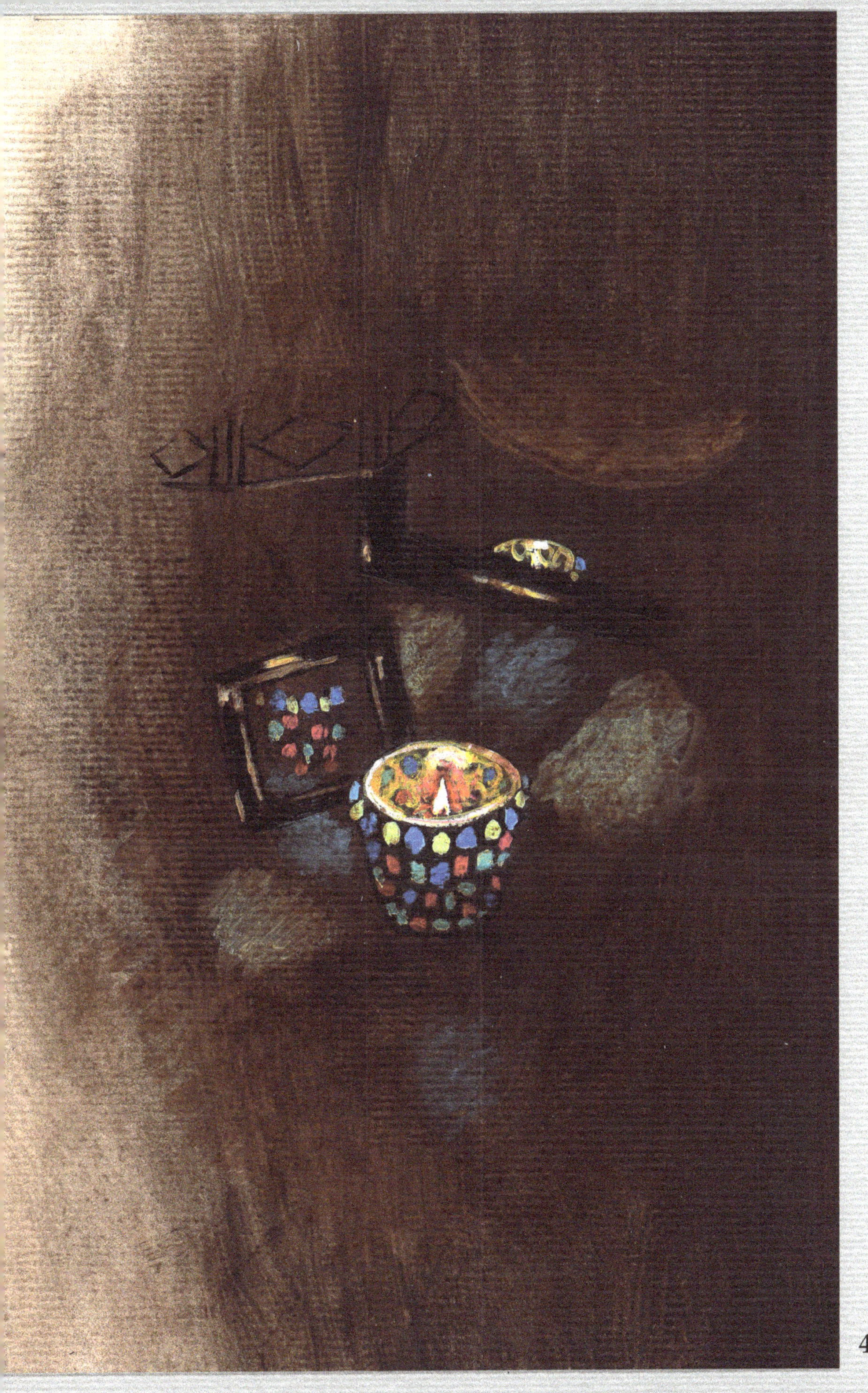

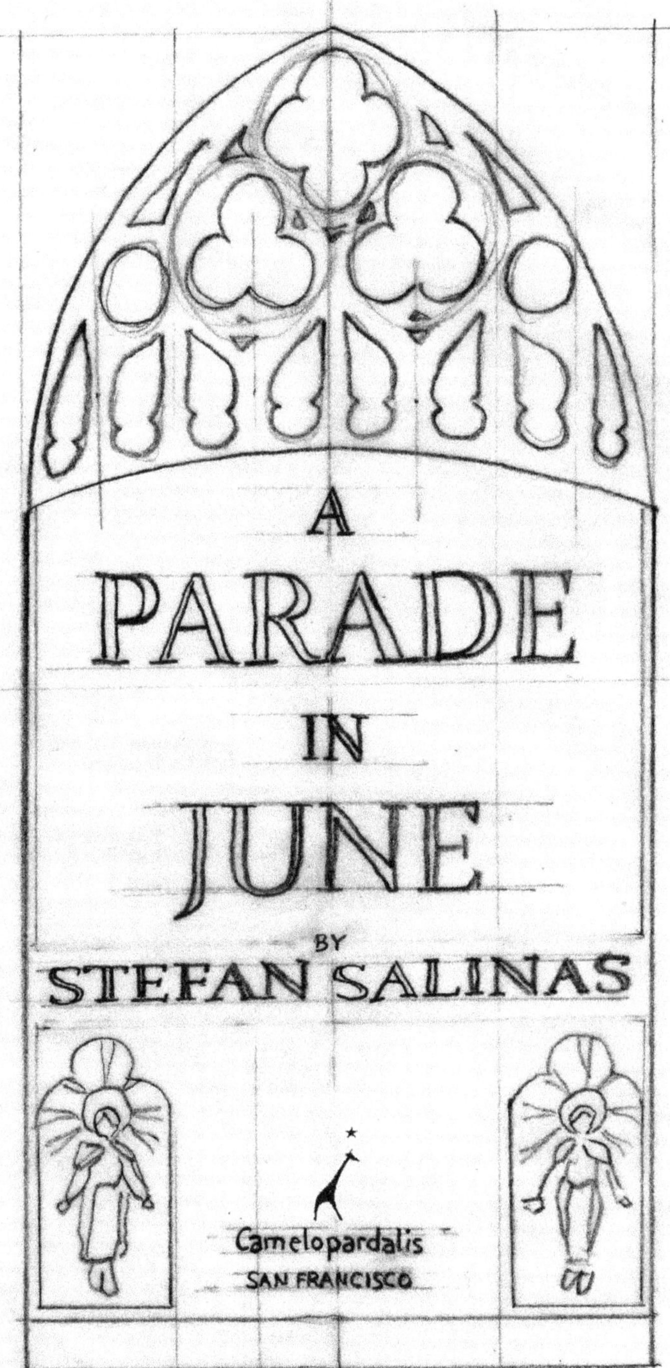
A
PARADE
IN
JUNE
BY
STEFAN SALINAS
Camelopardalis
SAN FRANCISCO

A man in his sixties said to me recently,
"THE GAY MEN OF MY GENERATION LEARNED TO LINK
SEX WITH FEAR."

PART 1

October: the first month of my Christian
Conversion process.

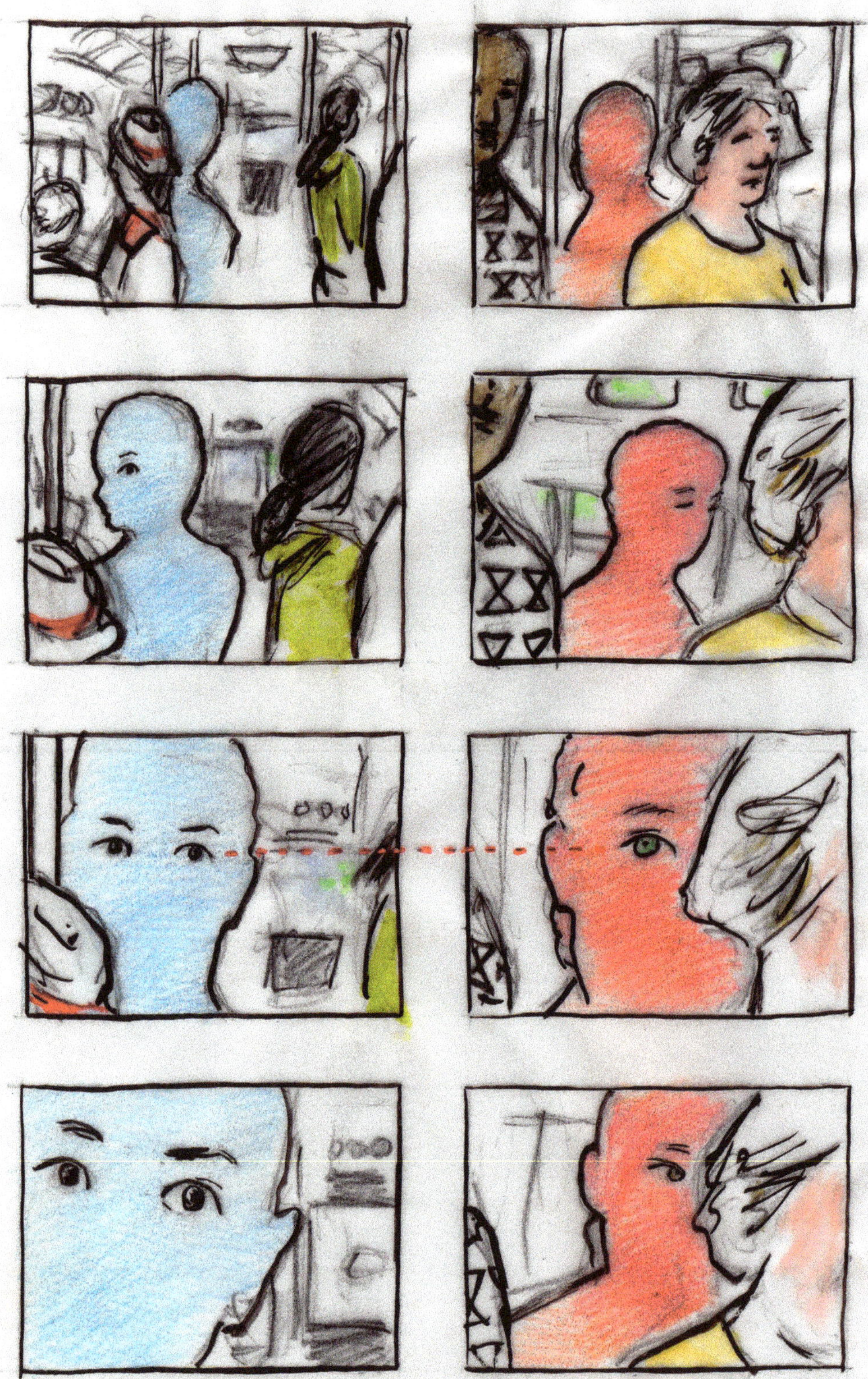

IT STRETCHES FROM FISHERMAN'S WARF TO THE
FERRY BUILDING, THEN DOWN MARKET ST. TO EUREKA
VALLEY (THE CASTRO).

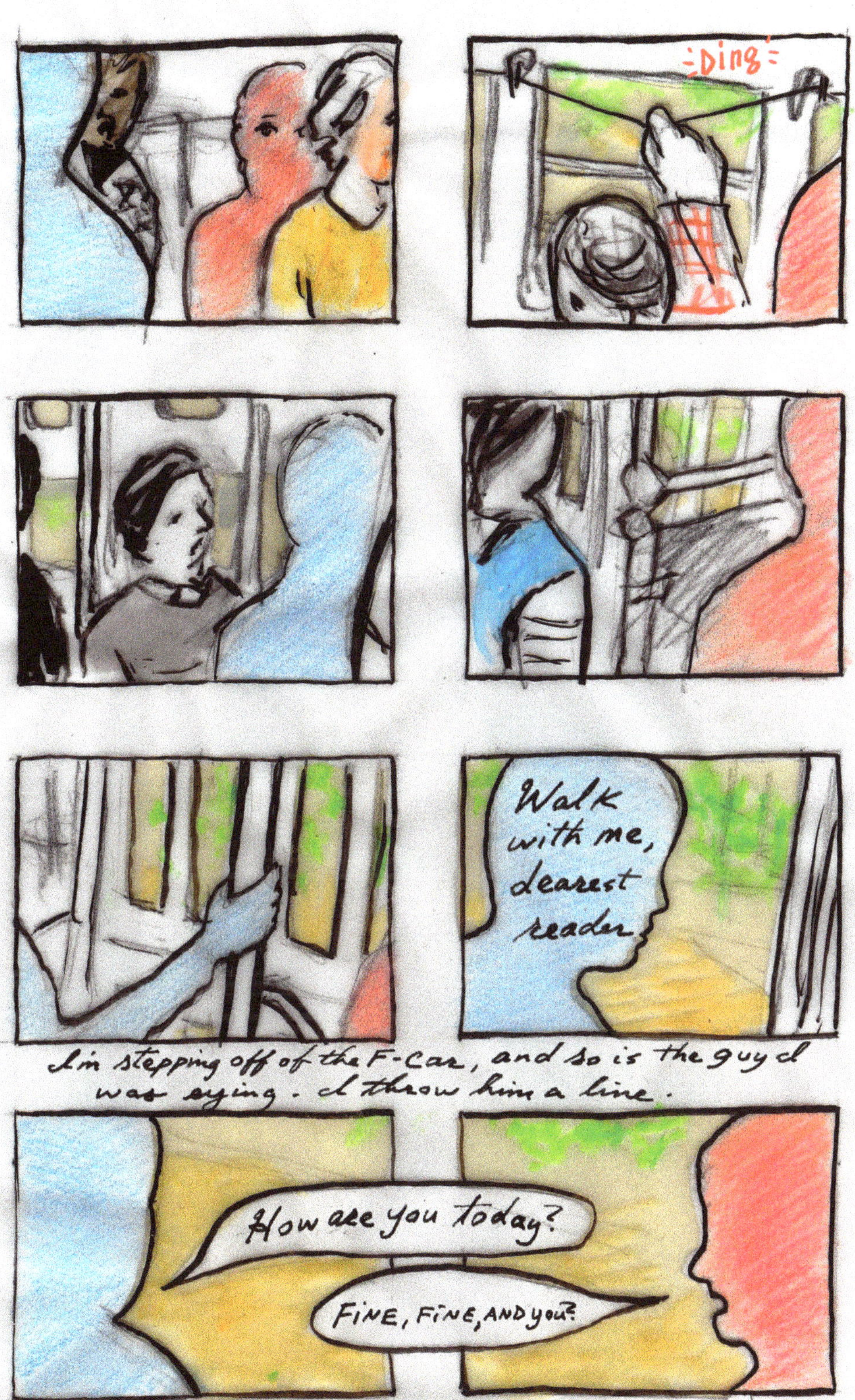

I'm stepping off of the F-Car, and so is the guy I was eying. I throw him a line.

He's just coming from a mass in the ___ district, at a church where I have friends.

He's set to go
for a long
walk,

so he agrees to
accompany me
while I run errands.
He's a fit, middle-aged man with an adorable,
thick Irish brogue.

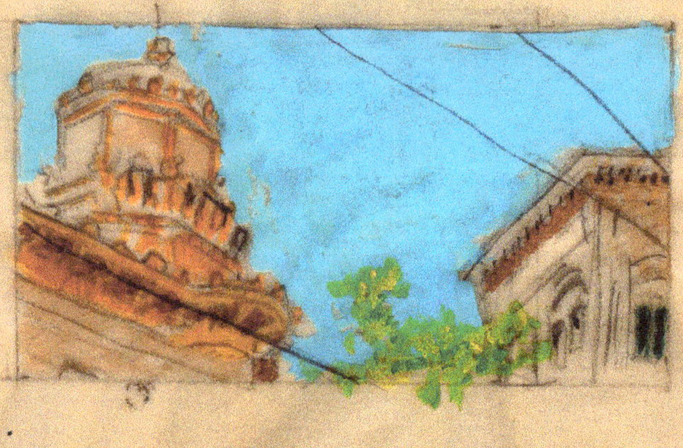

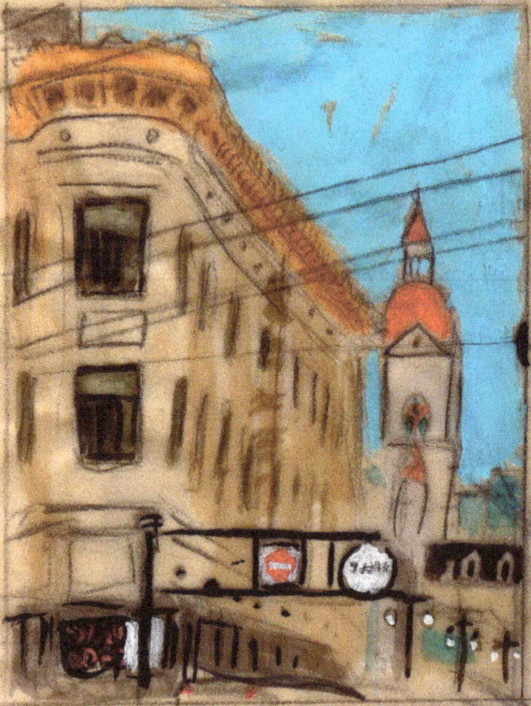

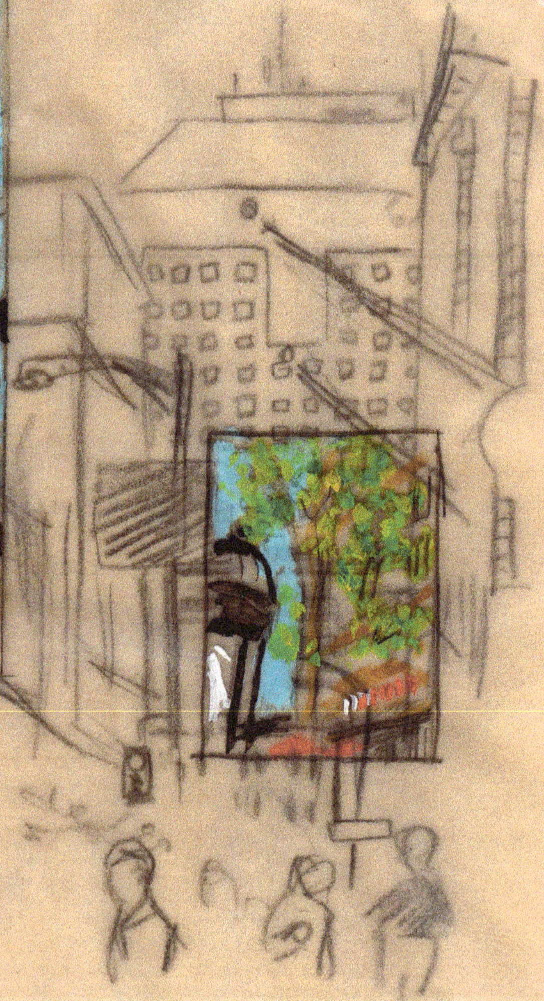

Oh,
and he's completely
in the closet.

Let's call him
PATRICK.

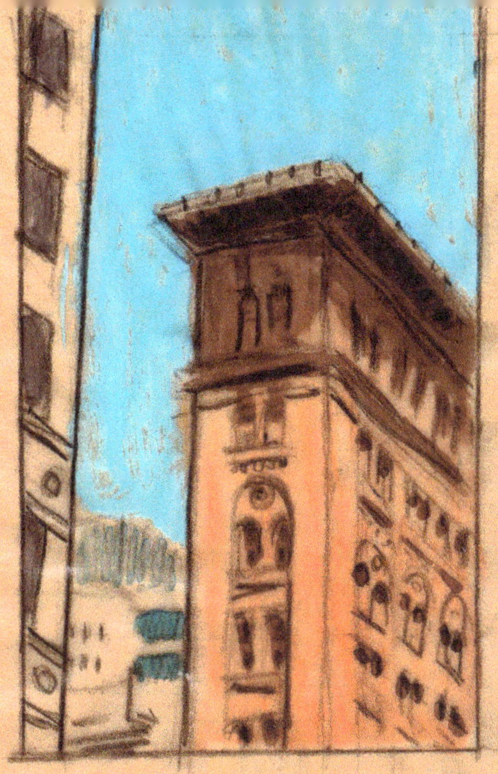

Quite a religious man,
Patrick attends mass daily and sometimes twice on Sundays.

Self-Solace?

His home parish is downtown, so we're heading there to peek inside. He's been in the states for over 2 decades, while his family resides in a rural Northern Ireland town.

He fears being out, even here ... here in the Gay Capital of California (?!)

ST. PATRICK'S CHURCH, ERECTED 1872.
FEATURED IN IT'S STAINED
GLASS ARE THE PATRON SAINTS OF THE
32 COUNTIES OF IRELAND.
THIS MAY OR MAY NOT BE THE
ACTUAL CHURCH WE ARE VISITING.

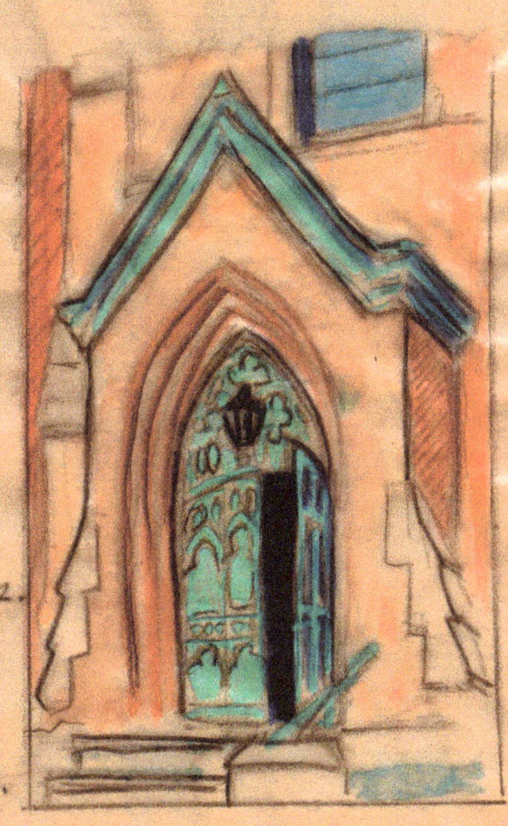

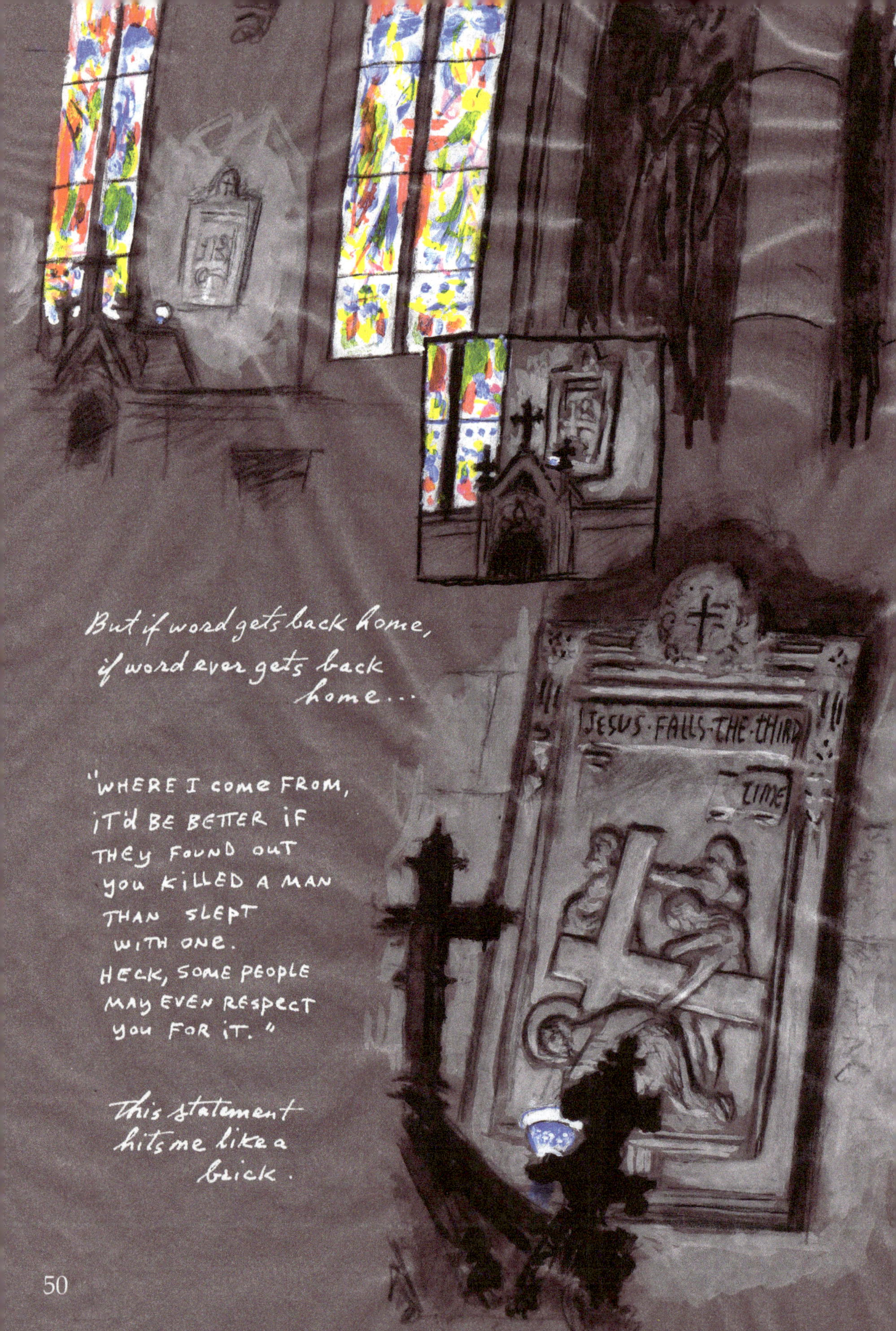
But if word gets back home,
if word ever gets back
home...

"WHERE I COME FROM,
iT'd BE BETTER IF
THEy FOUND OUT
you KILLED A MAN
THAN SLEPT
WITH ONE.
HECK, SOME PEOPLE
MAY EVEN RESPECT
you FOR iT."

this statement
hits me like a
brick.

JESUS · FALLS · THE · THIRD
TIME

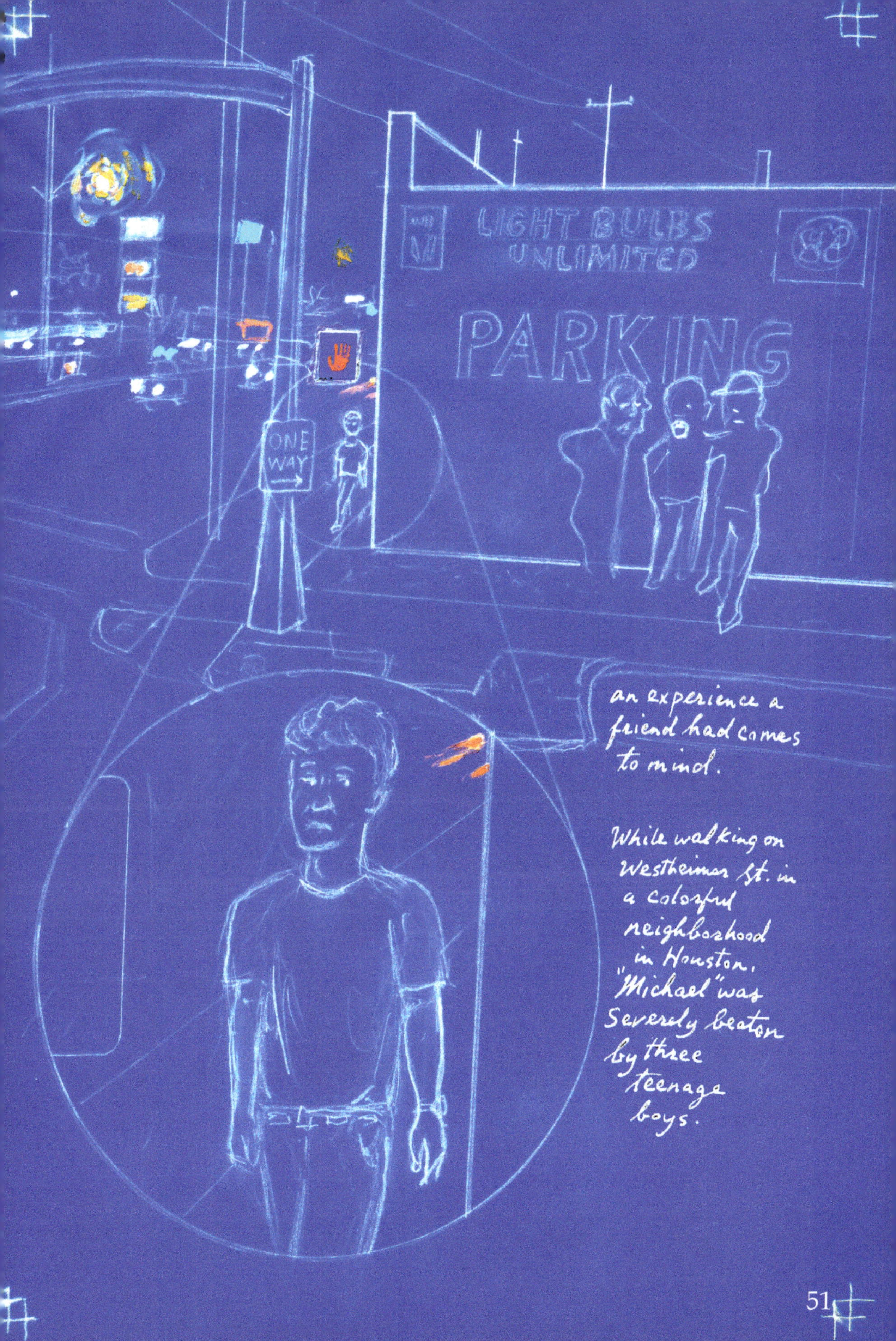

an experience a friend had comes to mind.

While walking on Westheimer St. in a colorful neighborhood in Houston, "Michael" was severely beaten by three teenage boys.

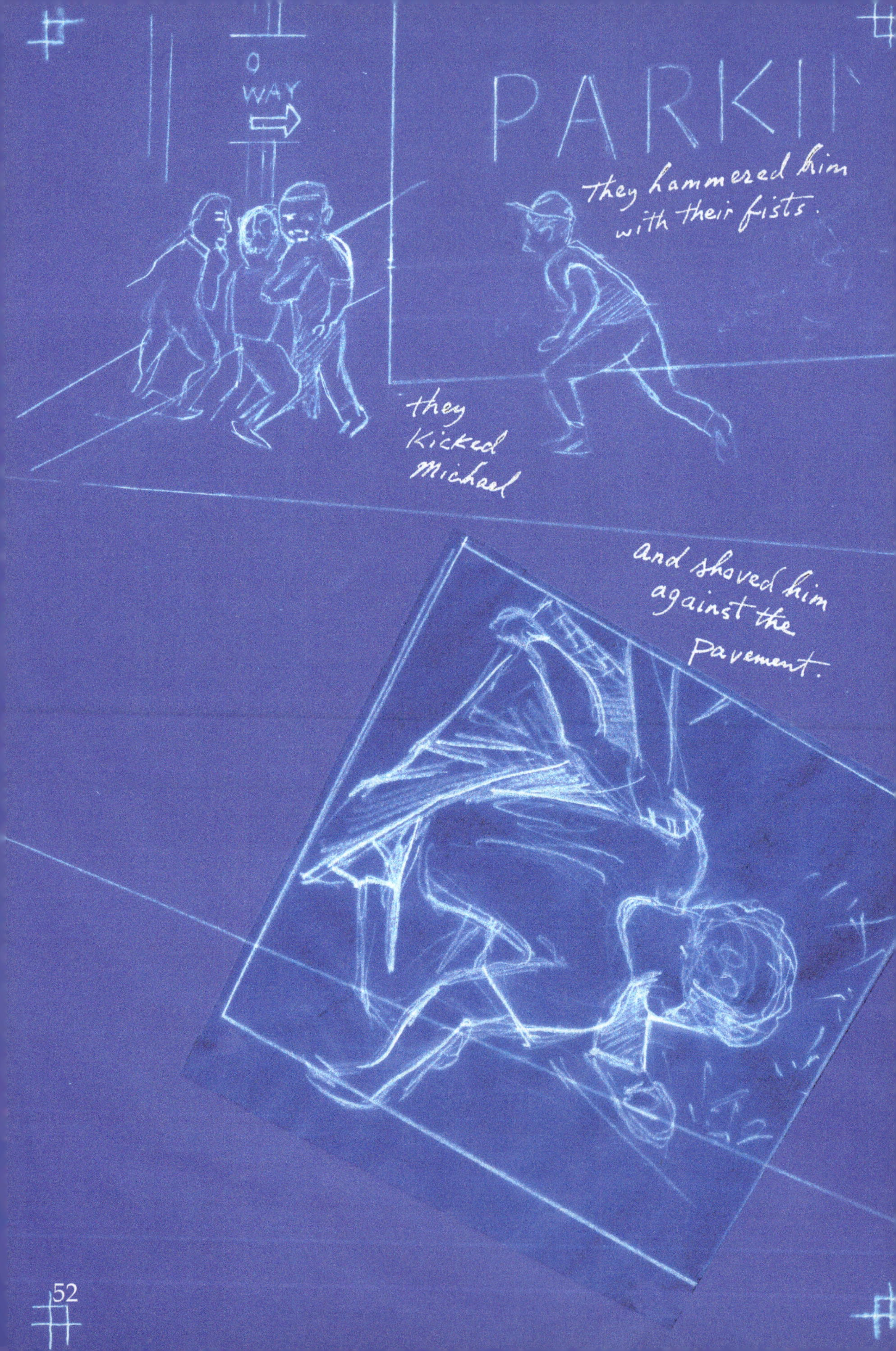
PARKIN
O
WAY
they hammered him
with their fists.
they
Kicked
Michael
and shoved him
against the
Pavement.
52

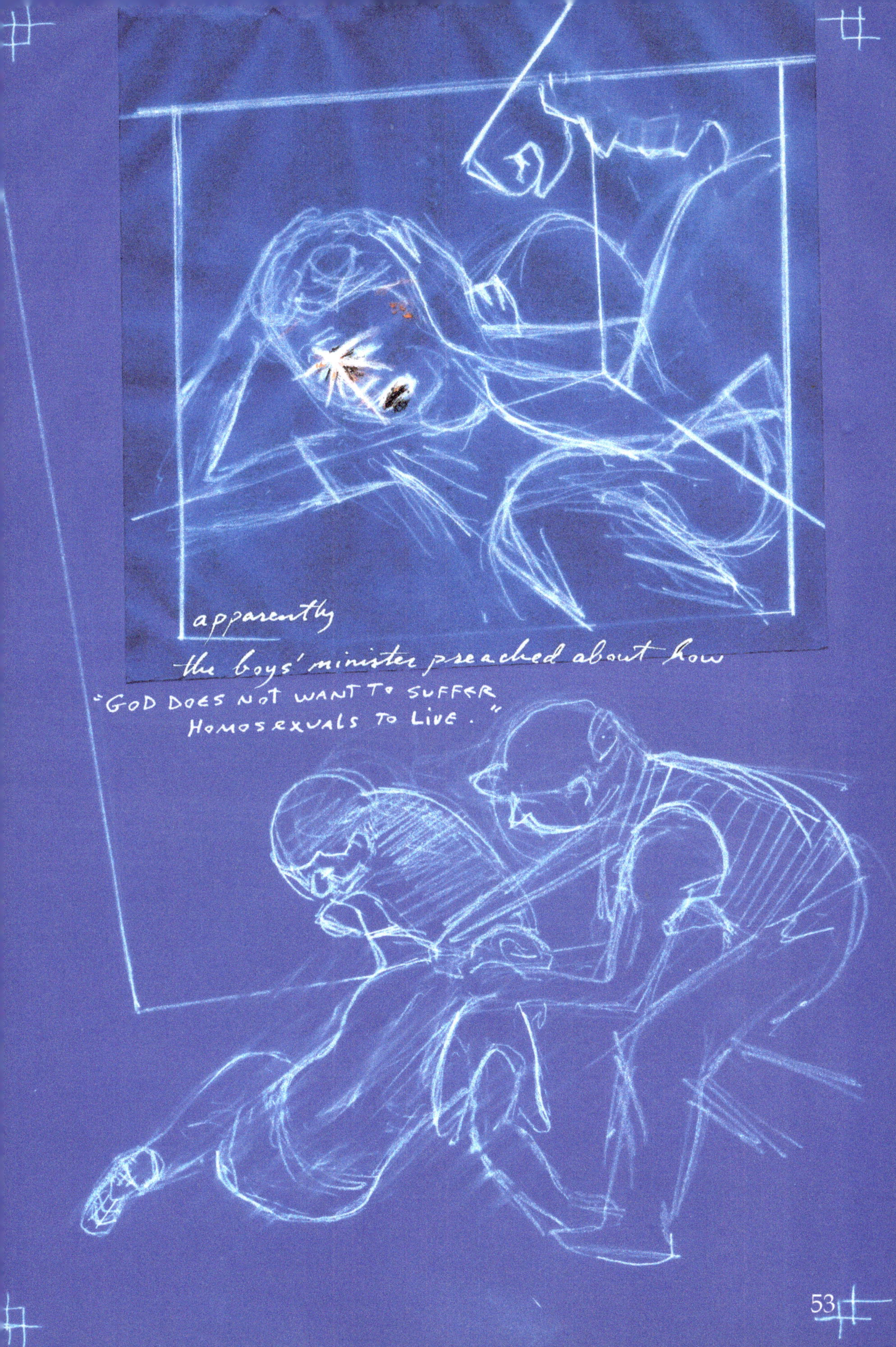

apparently
the boys' minister preached about how
"GOD DOES NOT WANT TO SUFFER
HOMOSEXUALS TO LIVE."
53

This occurred
several years
ago,
and to
this day he
still can't
hear out of
his left ear.
Is it any wonder Michael's
now a Buddhist? *

* A CORRECTION: AT THE TIME OF THE ATTACK,
MICHAEL HAD ALREADY BEEN A PRACTICING BUDDHIST FOR
8 YEARS. HE ADDS, "It was my Buddhist practice
that helped me overcome my fear of
being around self-identified christians, because I
set about to chant for the three boys
who attacked me."

My next task is to photograph a church
    for a book.

Back to my new friend.

We're sitting in a nearby café

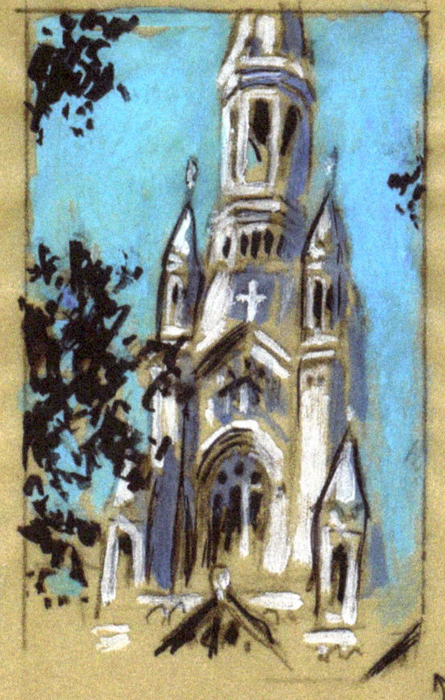

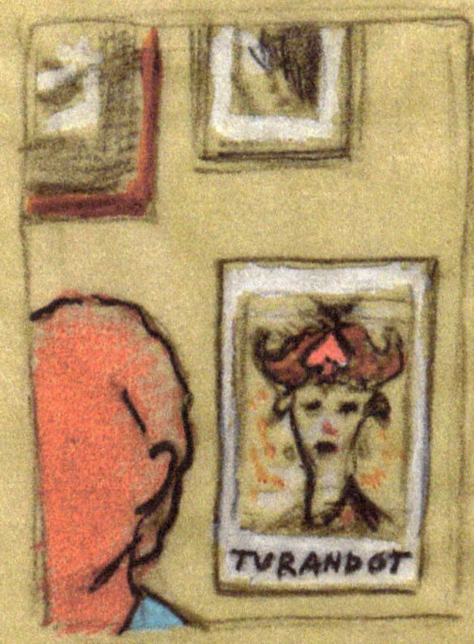

Ss. PETER & PAUL CHURCH, Est 1884. 1924.
A VERSE FROM DANTE'S PARADISO GRACES
IT'S FAÇADE: LA GLORIA DI COLUI CHE TUTTO
MUOVE PER L'UNIVERSO PENETRA E
RISPLENDA — THE GLORY OF HIM WHO
MOVES ALL THINGS PENETRATES, AND
GLOWS THROUGHOUT THE UNIVERSE.

Patrick confides,
    "I ONLY MEET MEN HERE AND THERE . . . IN PARKS,
BOOKSTORES, STAIRWELLS.
    IN A CONFESSIONAL, I REVEALED MY SECRET."

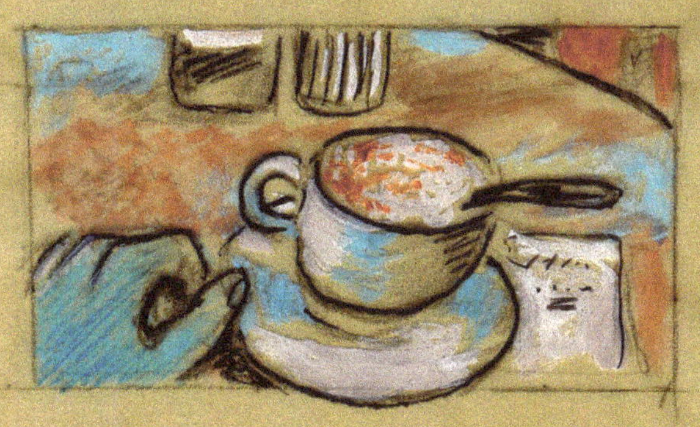

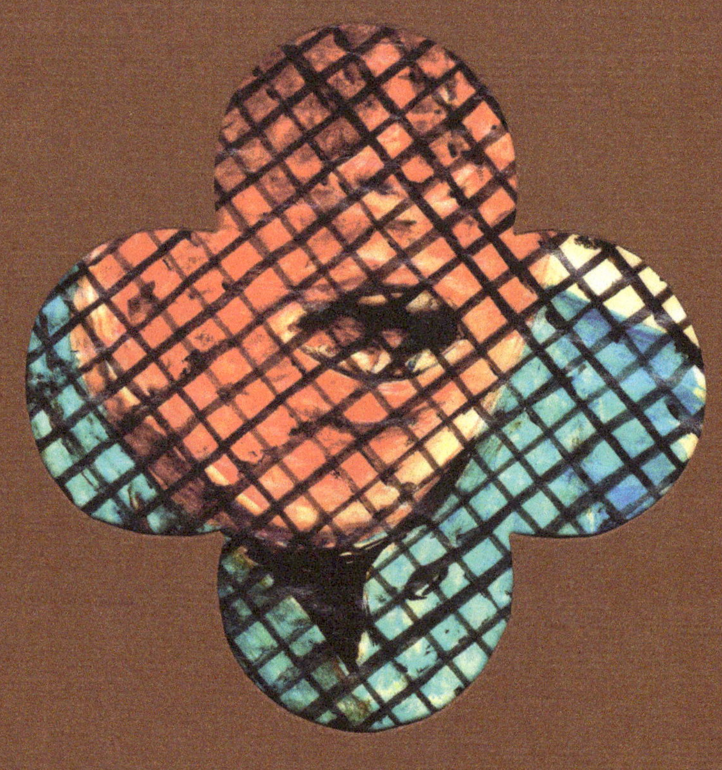

"I SAID, 'FATHER, I CAN'T HELP IT. I CAN'T SEEM TO
CHANGE IT. I AM ATTRACTED TO MEN, BUT I KNOW
I SHOULDN'T BE.'

AND THE PRIEST REPLIED,

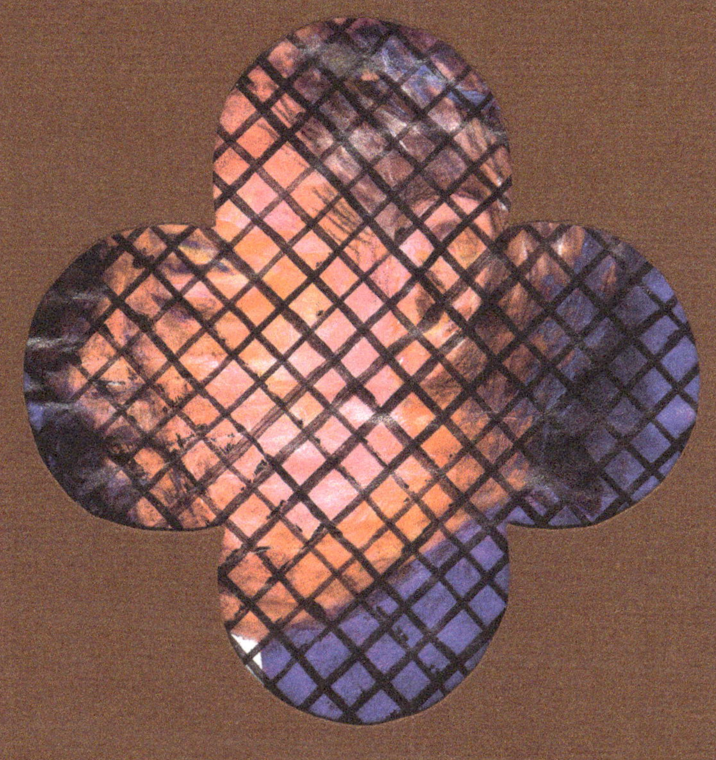

'My son, like it or not, God made each of us the way
we are. If you like men, then you must accept this.
Seek out a healthy, committed relationship.
This is very important for your personal growth.
Go on a proper date with a man.' "

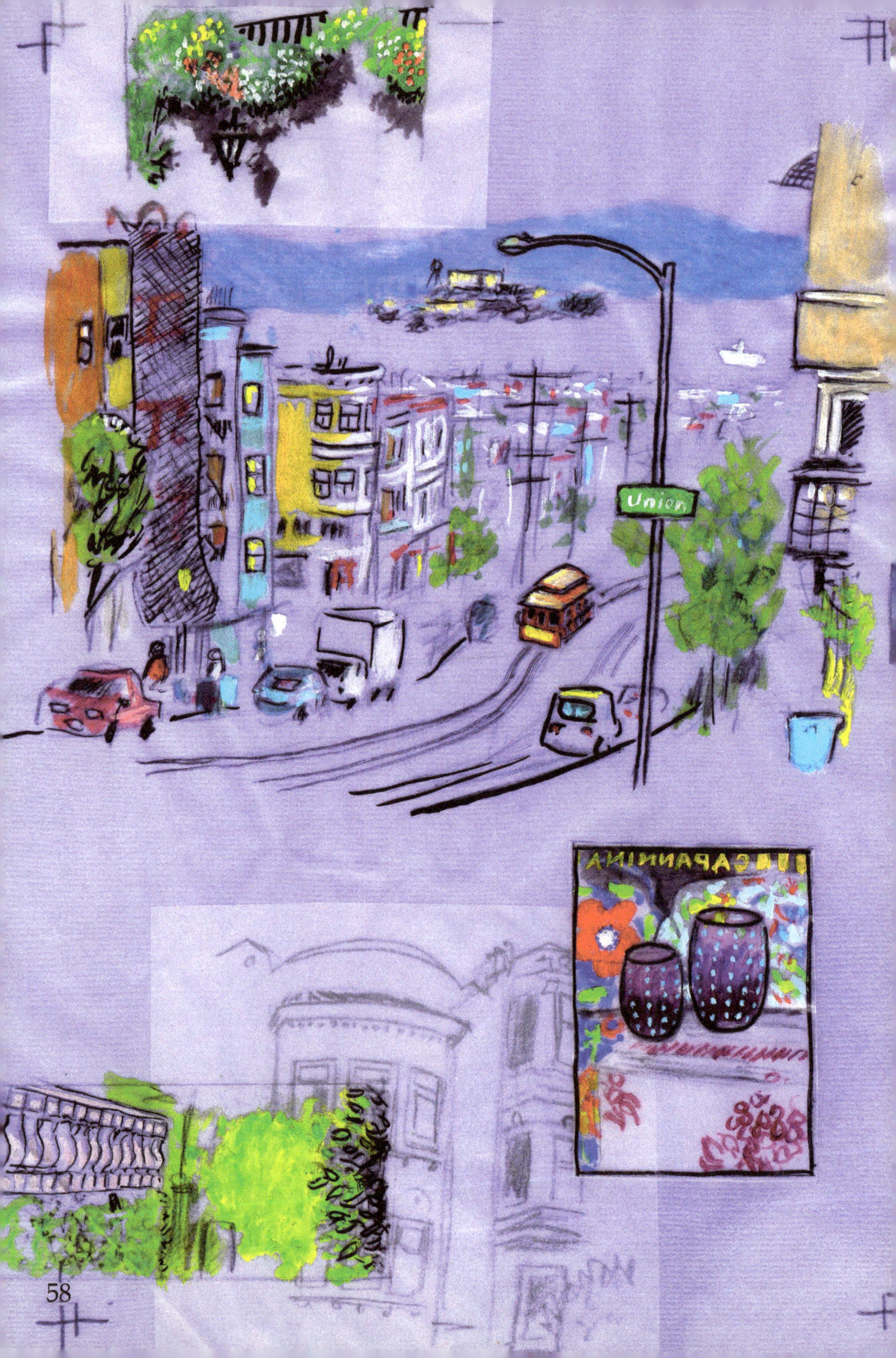

Union

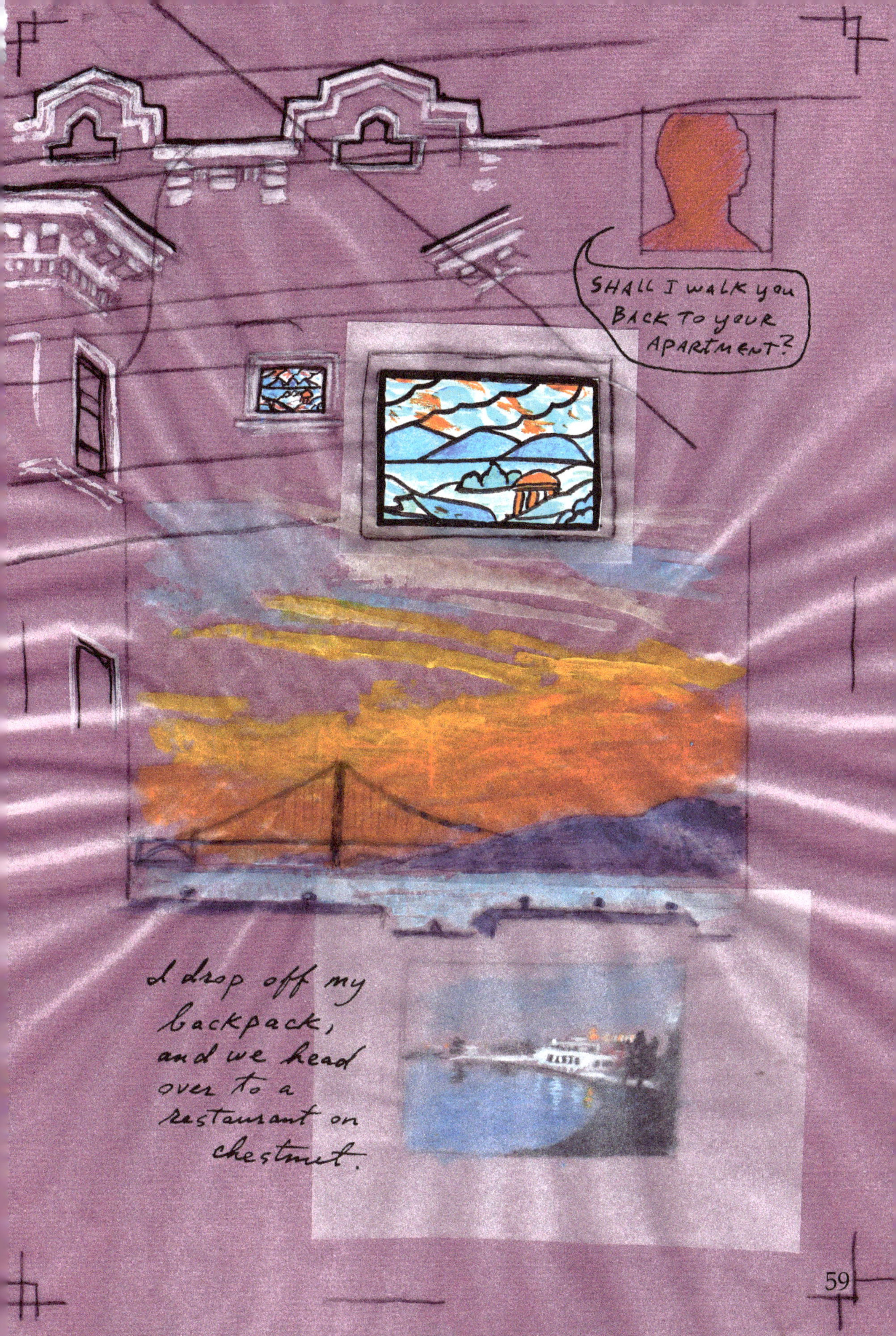
SHALL I WALK YOU
BACK TO YOUR
APARTMENT?
I drop off my
backpack,
and we head
over to a
restaurant on
chestnut.

And now we're strolling near the docks.
We sit against a low wall and hold each other.
Several couples walk by, taking in the
romantic evening.   He kisses me,

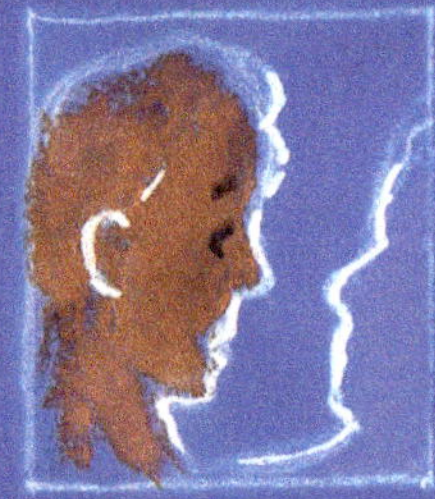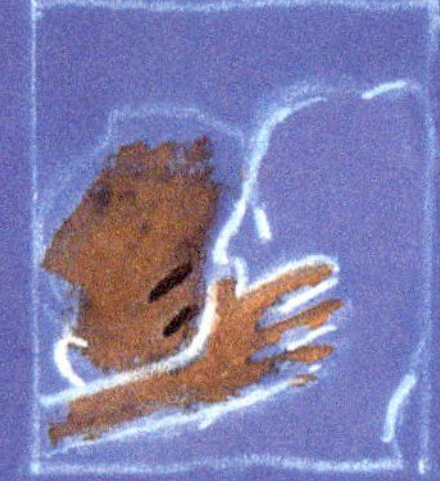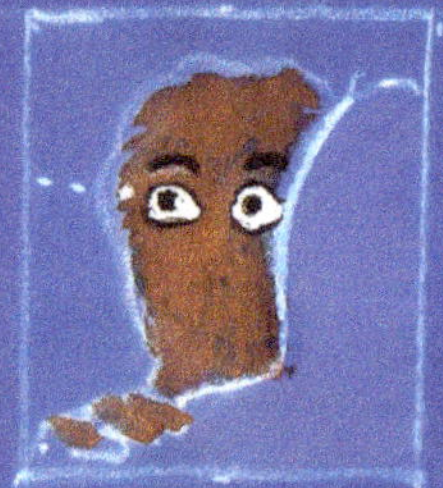

and kisses me some more.
We embrace each other tighter, and then
he peeks to see if anybody is looking at us.
We resume, and then...

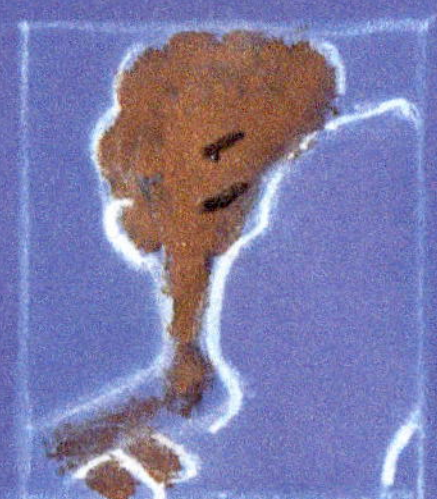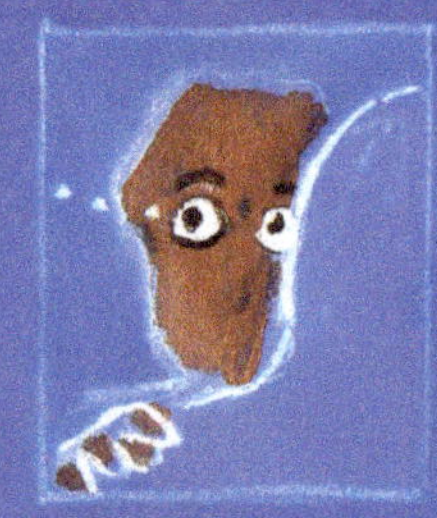

I stroke his neck
while I assure him
"What are you
afraid of?

We're safe here. We're not in the Central
Valley. Nobody cares in this area.
We're safe here. We're safe here...

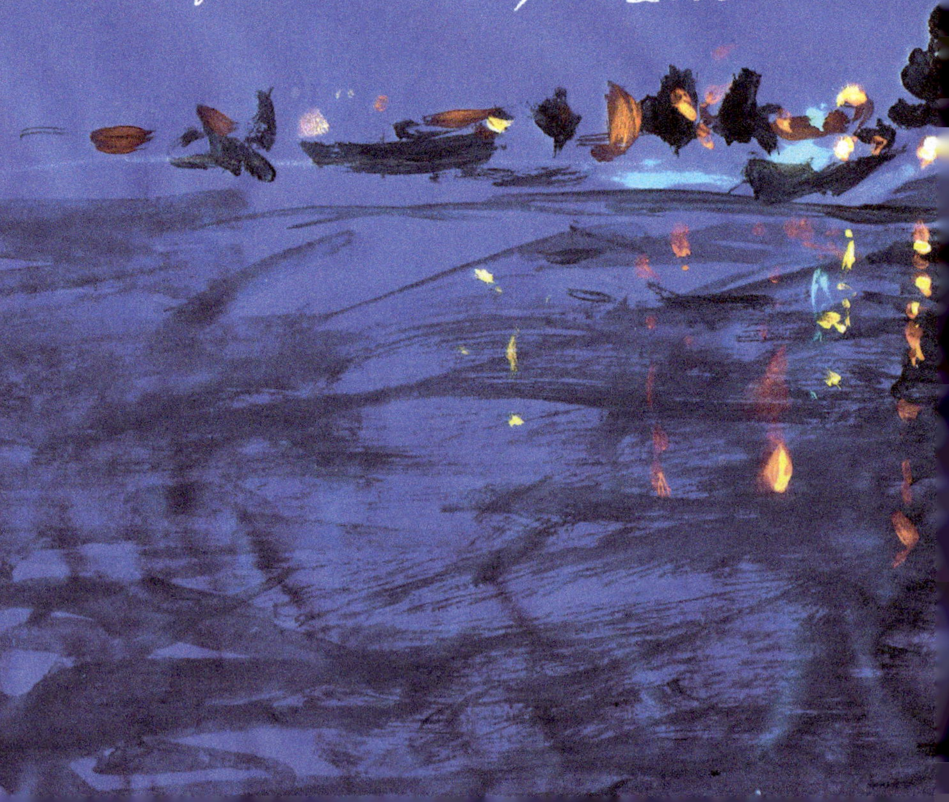

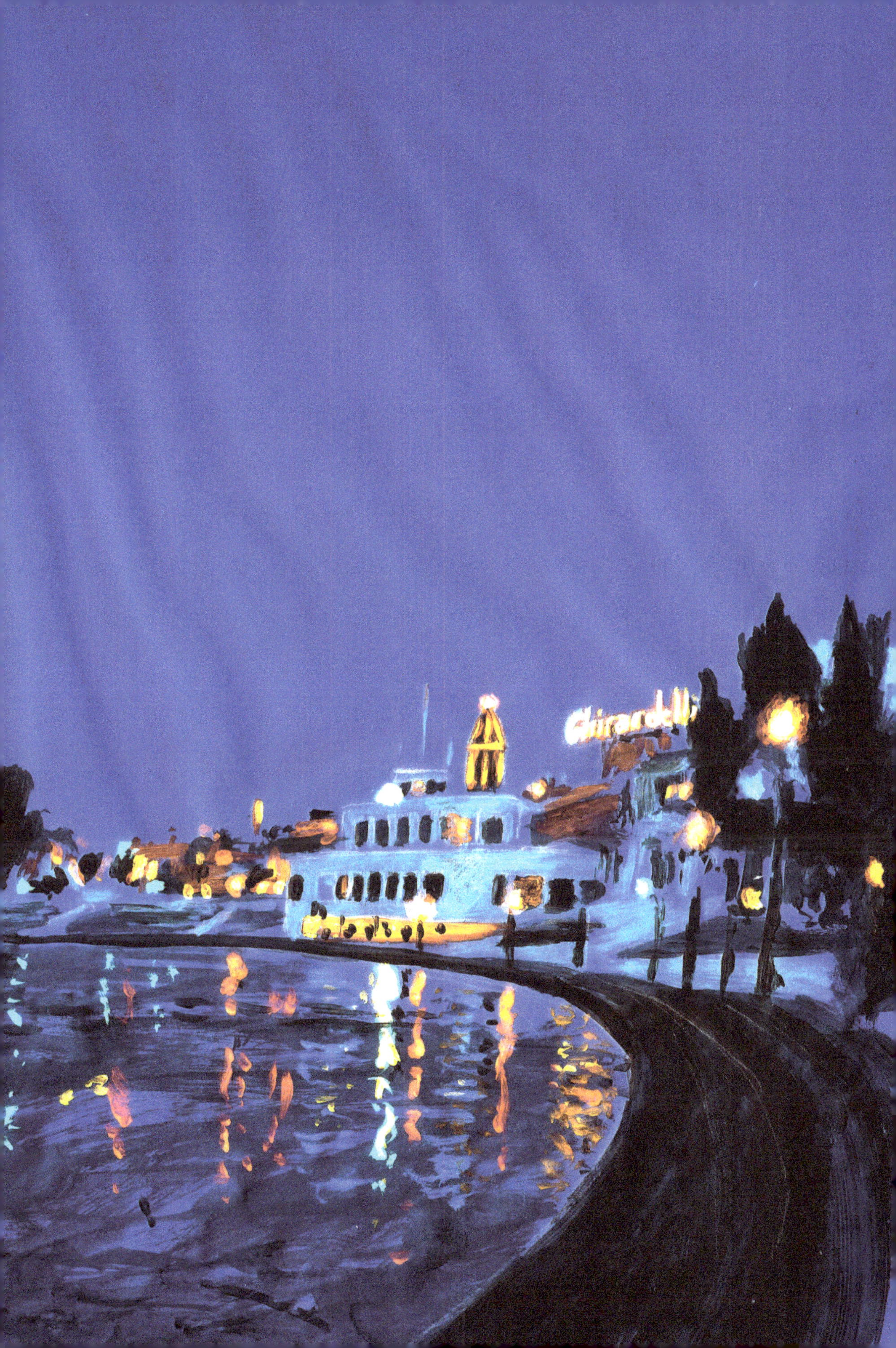

Ghirardelli

It's time for a confession.
You'll be the priest
and
I'll be the confessor.

Let's turn the clock back
to June, before my "Move to Rome"; before
I decided to become a Catholic.

It was the Saturday night of
Gay Pride weekend.

PART 2

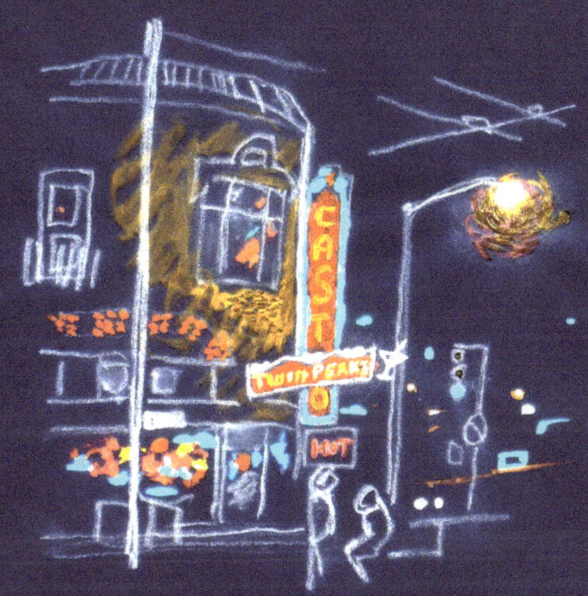

The crowd in the bar I visited was
lively and colorful, as would be
expected — excited and jumping with
anticipation.

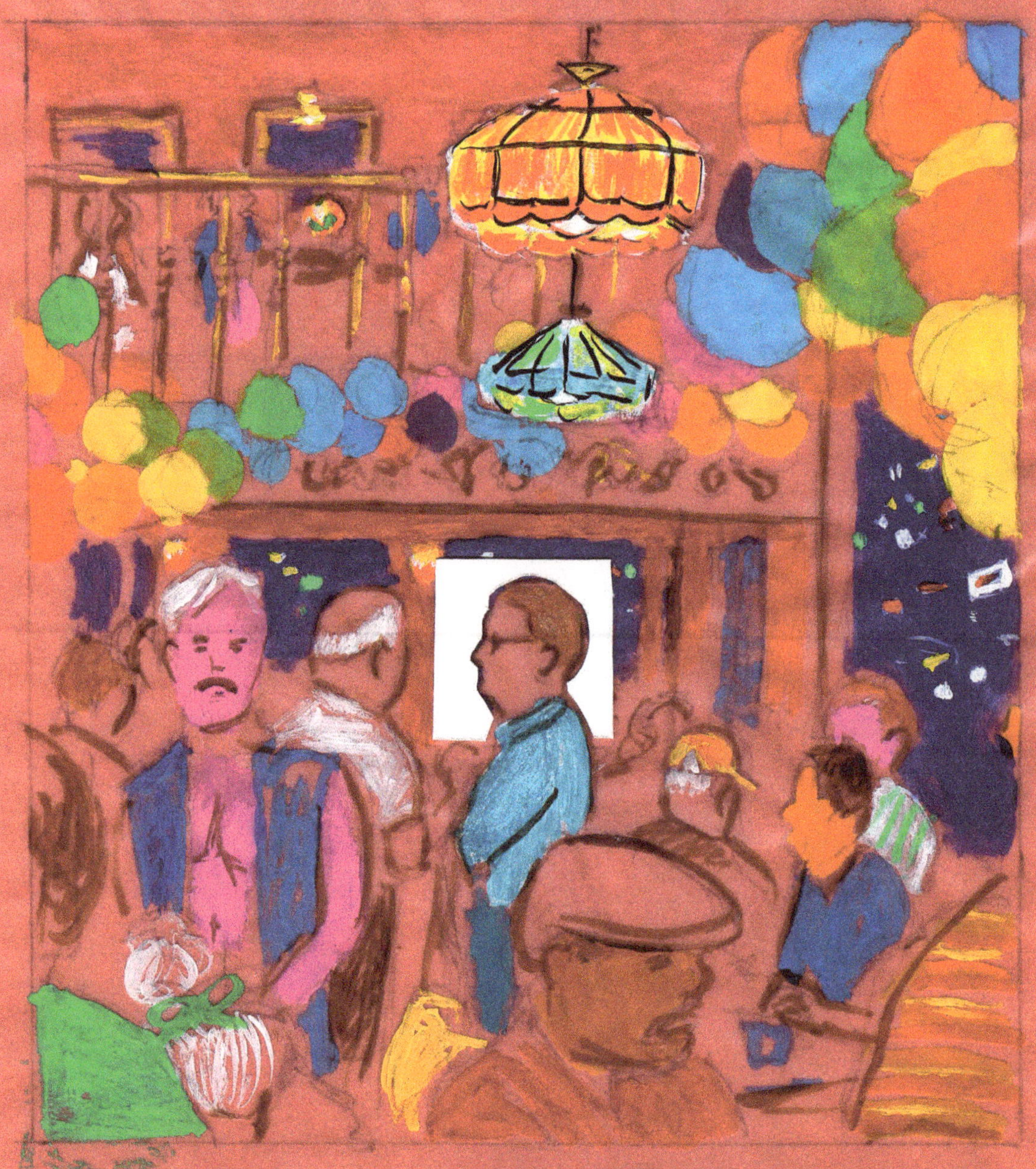

TWIN PEAKS IS A CULTURAL LANDMARK ON THE CORNER
OF 17TH ST. AND CASTRO. IT IS THE FIRST GAY BAR IN
AMERICA TO FEATURE WINDOWS.

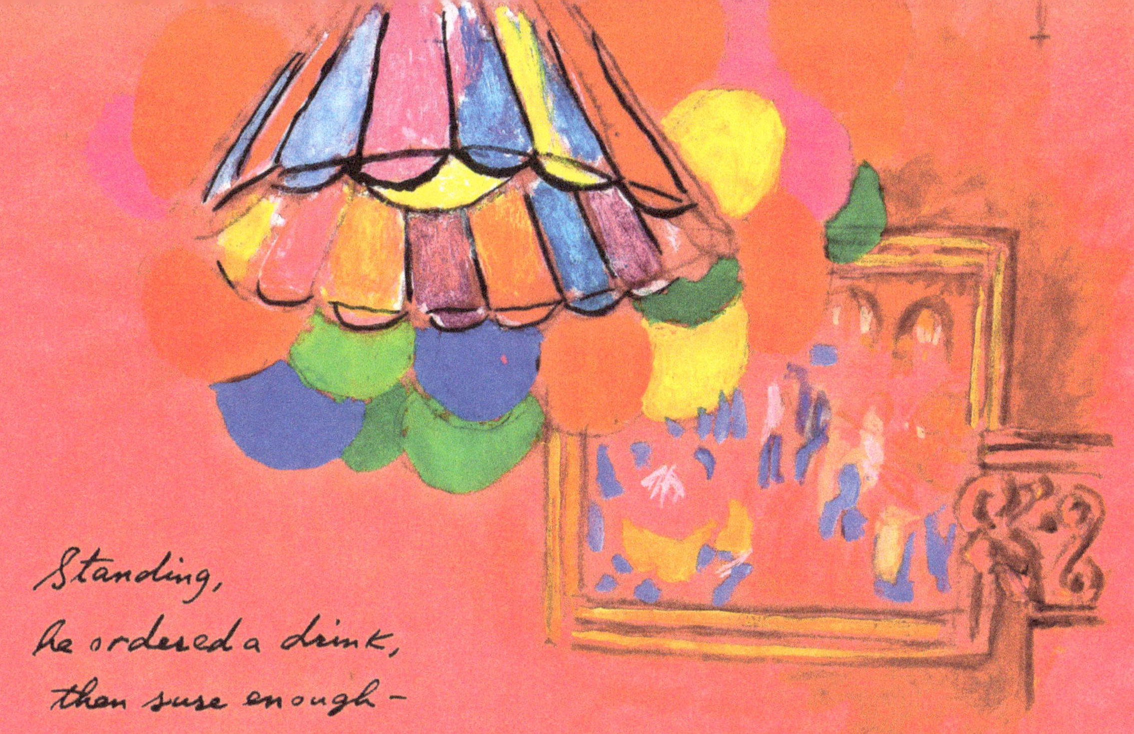

Standing,
he ordered a drink,
then sure enough —

a Sprite. Good sign. Late fifties, tall, large frame, with a NICE smile and sincere eyes. "John" is from the Bible Belt, and his large, Southern hand cradled mine. It was warm and gentle ... warm and gentle and Married!

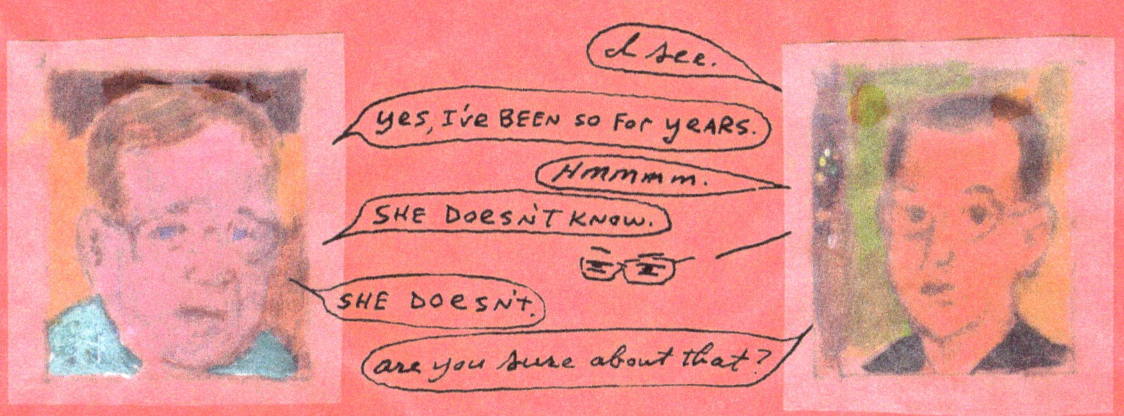

There are issues, and John explained them to me. He continued, "WE DON'T SLEEP TOGETHER ...
NO CHILDREN. I LOVE HER," he sighed, "I LOVE HER VERY MUCH. SHE'S MY ANCHOR AND MY FRIEND FOR LIFE.

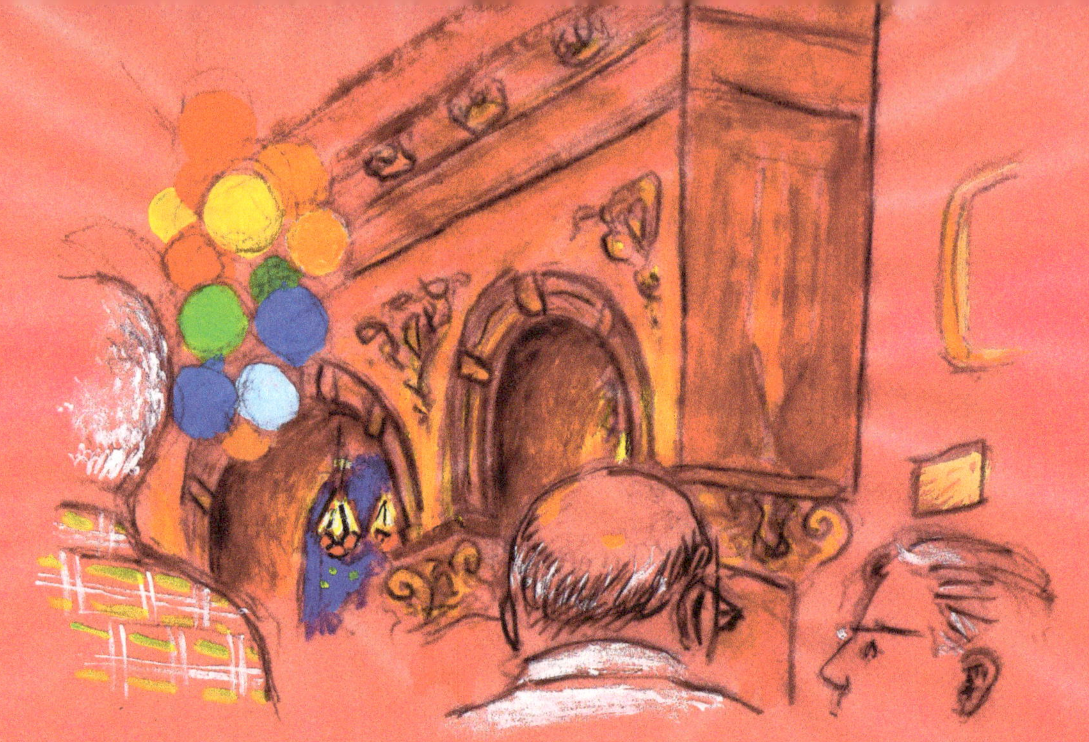

He went on to tell me about their careers and his many business trips (and now here — how convenient!)

Leave it to me to bring up religion to every Tom, Dick and Harry.

Mine was Unitarianism. He's a Baptist who's very involved in his church — a faithful congregant and dedicated volunteer; a helping hand to others.

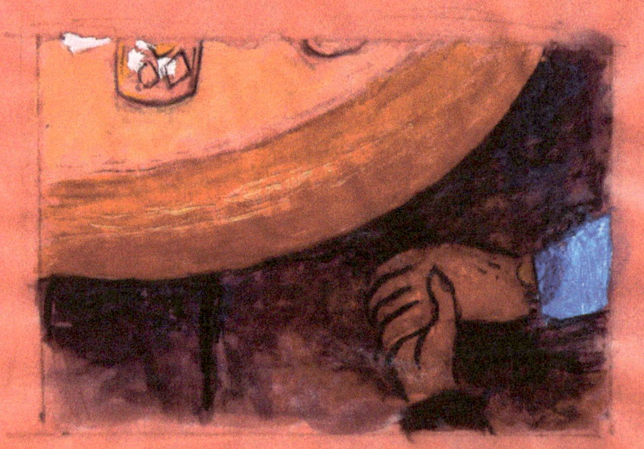

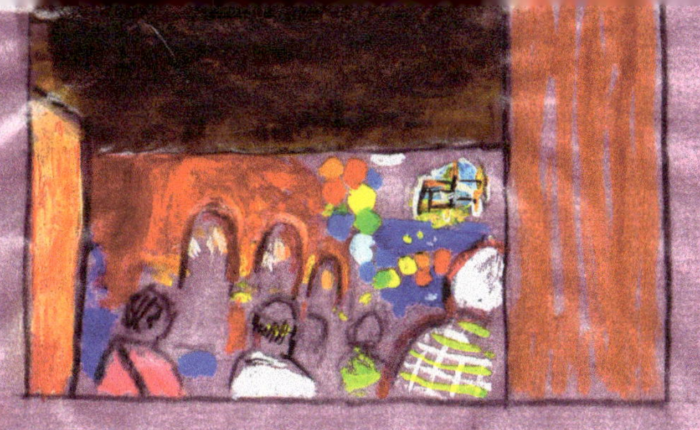

John couldn't be up too late. He would have an early morning meeting, and I had a lecture to attend, so we continued our conversation in a cab to his hotel.

On the way, we passed Glide Memorial Methodist and I mentioned that I'd heard that they have really lively services which he may want to attend. He knew about it and said it used to be a Catholic church. This turned out to be false information, but that idea intrigues me: a transformative house of worship.

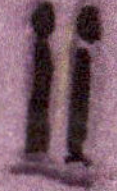

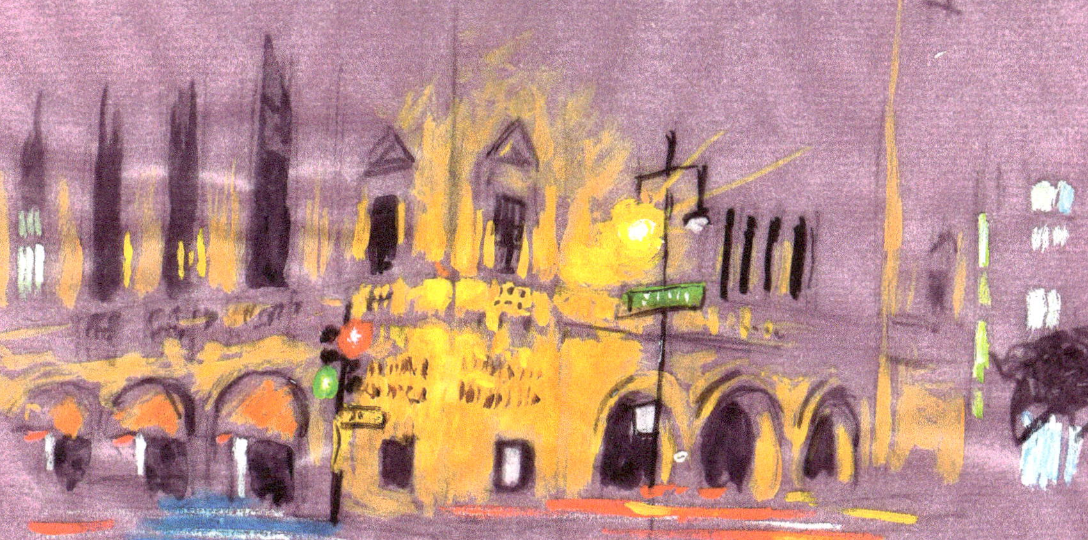

Who does this lovely
giant hold when he's
not away from home?
a hunting buddy lives in a neighboring County...

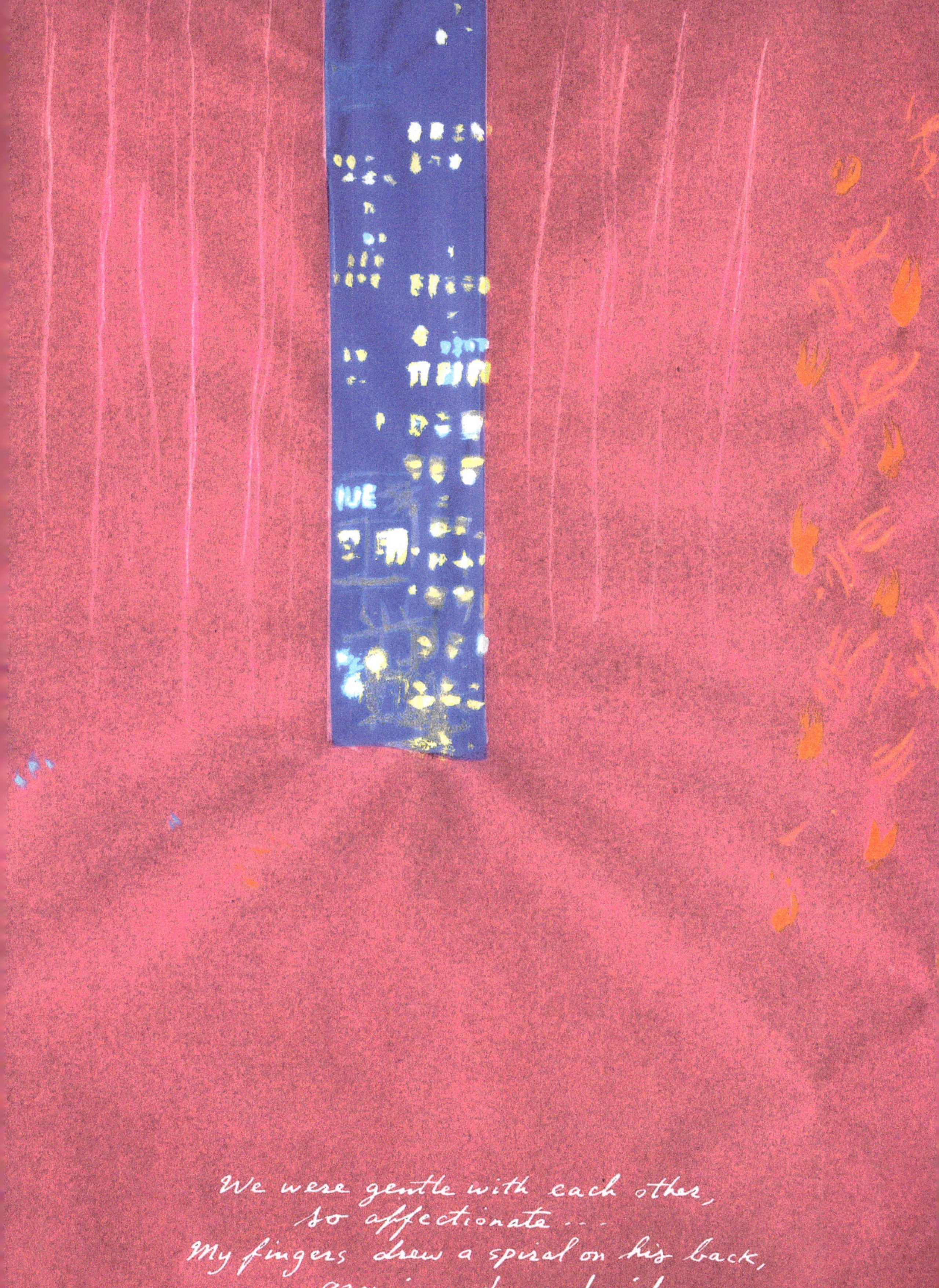

We were gentle with each other,
so affectionate . . .
My fingers drew a spiral on his back,
growing wider and wider . . .

That night, a guilt dream:

we were hiding from his wife
and her friend as they walked
out of their guest house
carrying paper plates and
other 4th of July supplies....

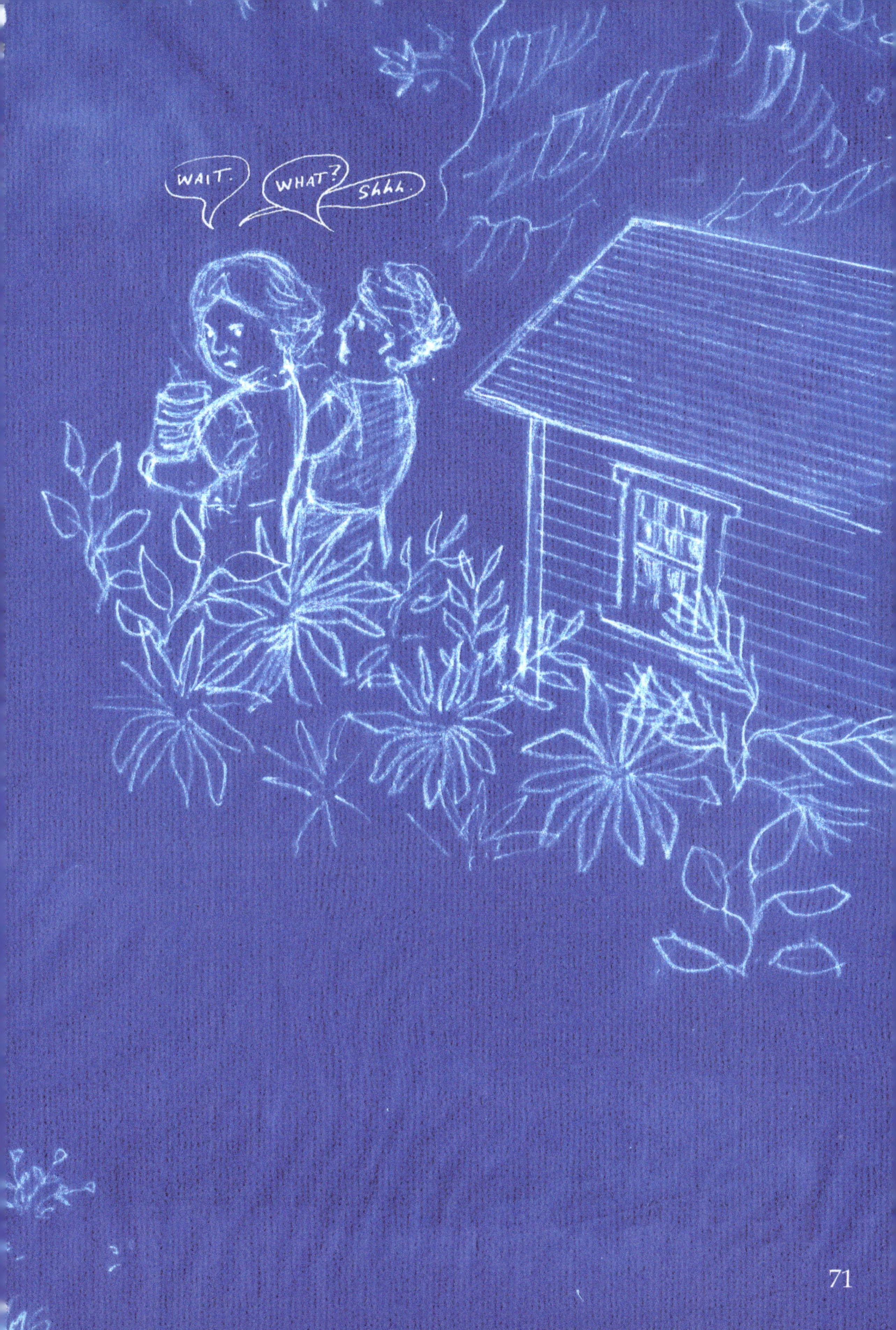

WAIT.
WHAT?
Shh.

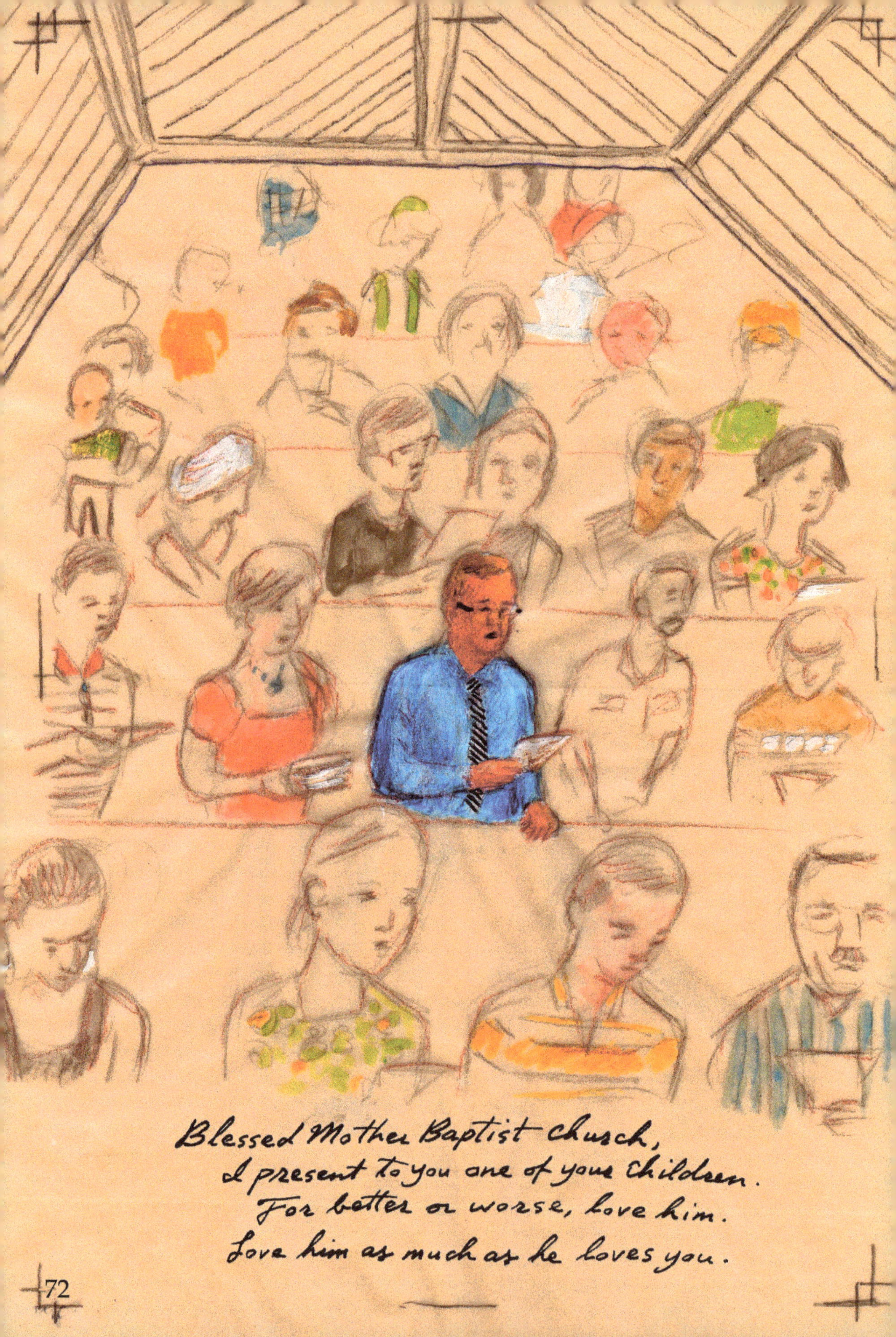

Blessed Mother Baptist Church,
I present to you one of your children.
For better or worse, love him.
Love him as much as he loves you.

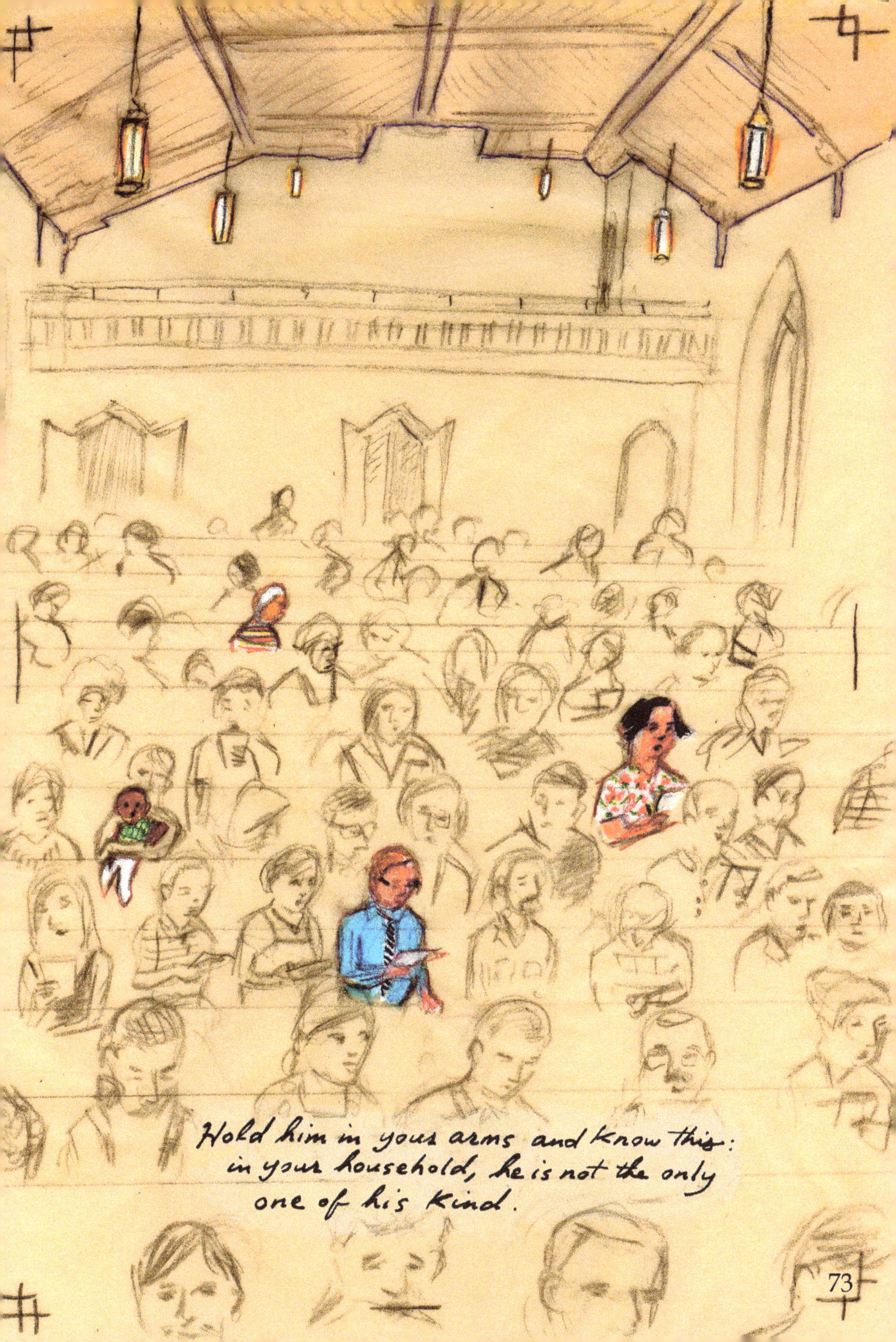

Hold him in your arms and know this:
in your household, he is not the only
one of his kind.

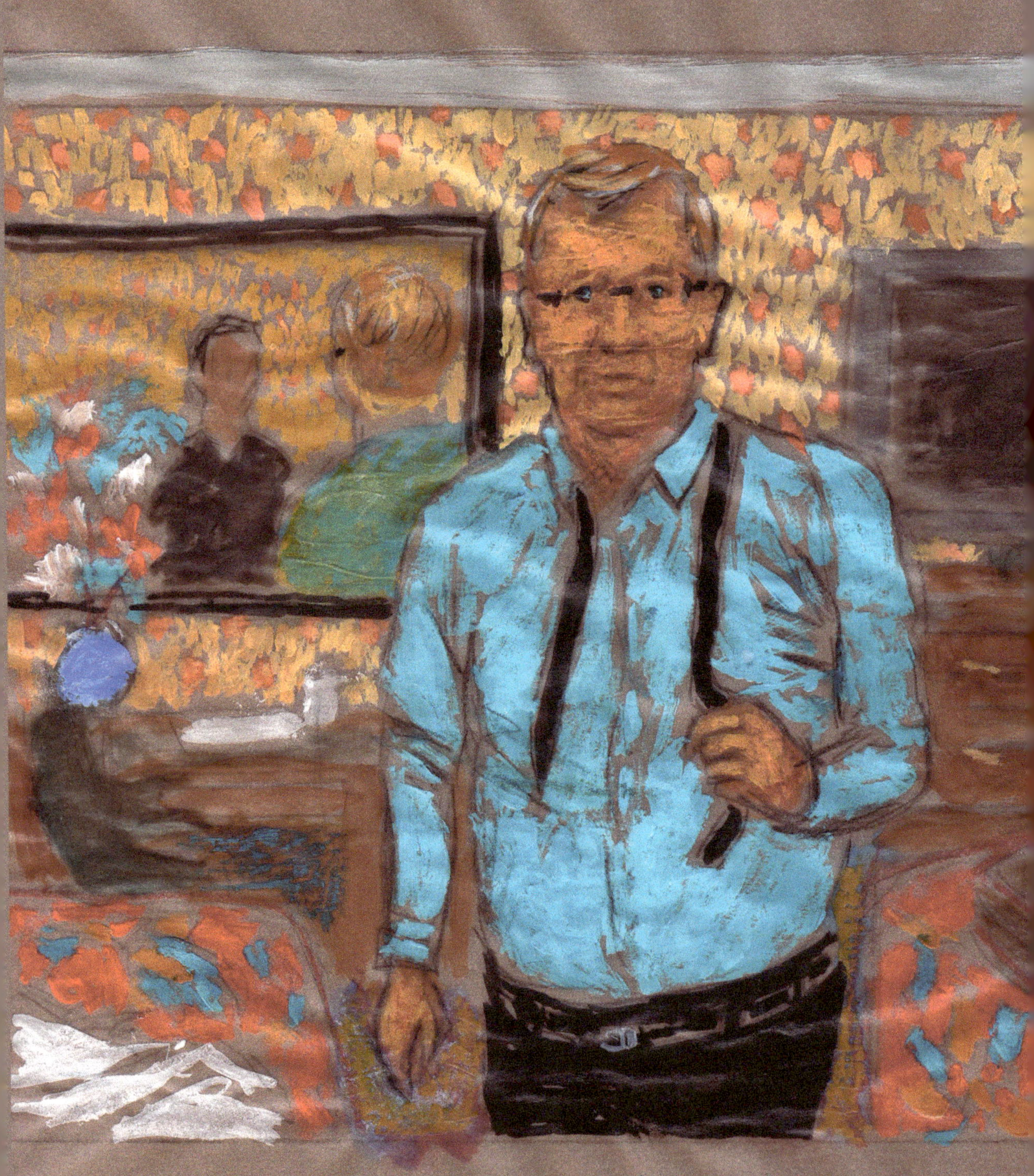

The next morning we chatted about hobbies while he packed his suitcase and suited up for work. It was too risky to exchange numbers or emails.

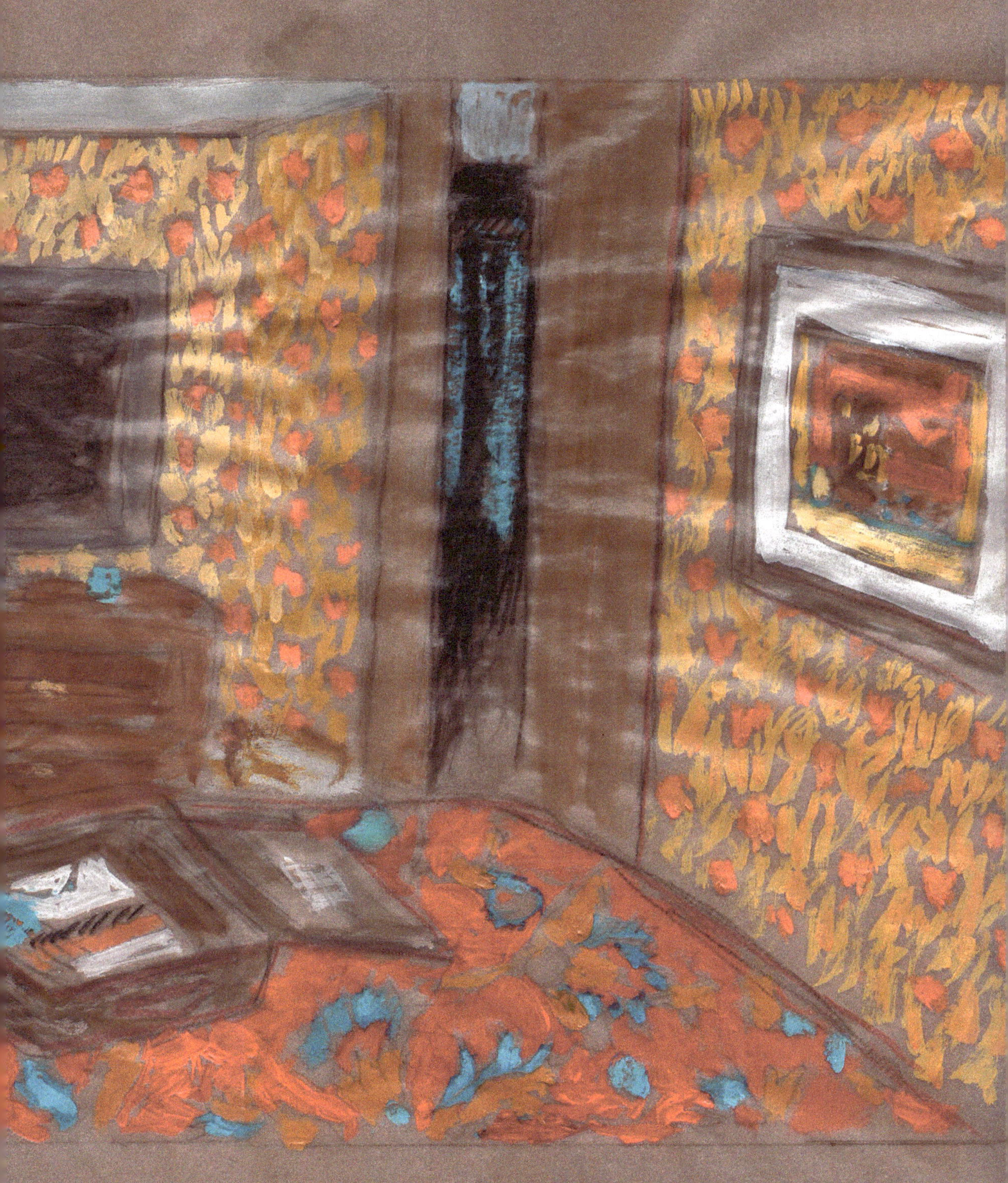

John paused while tying his tie.
"MAY I ASK YOU, WHAT IS YOUR FULL NAME?"

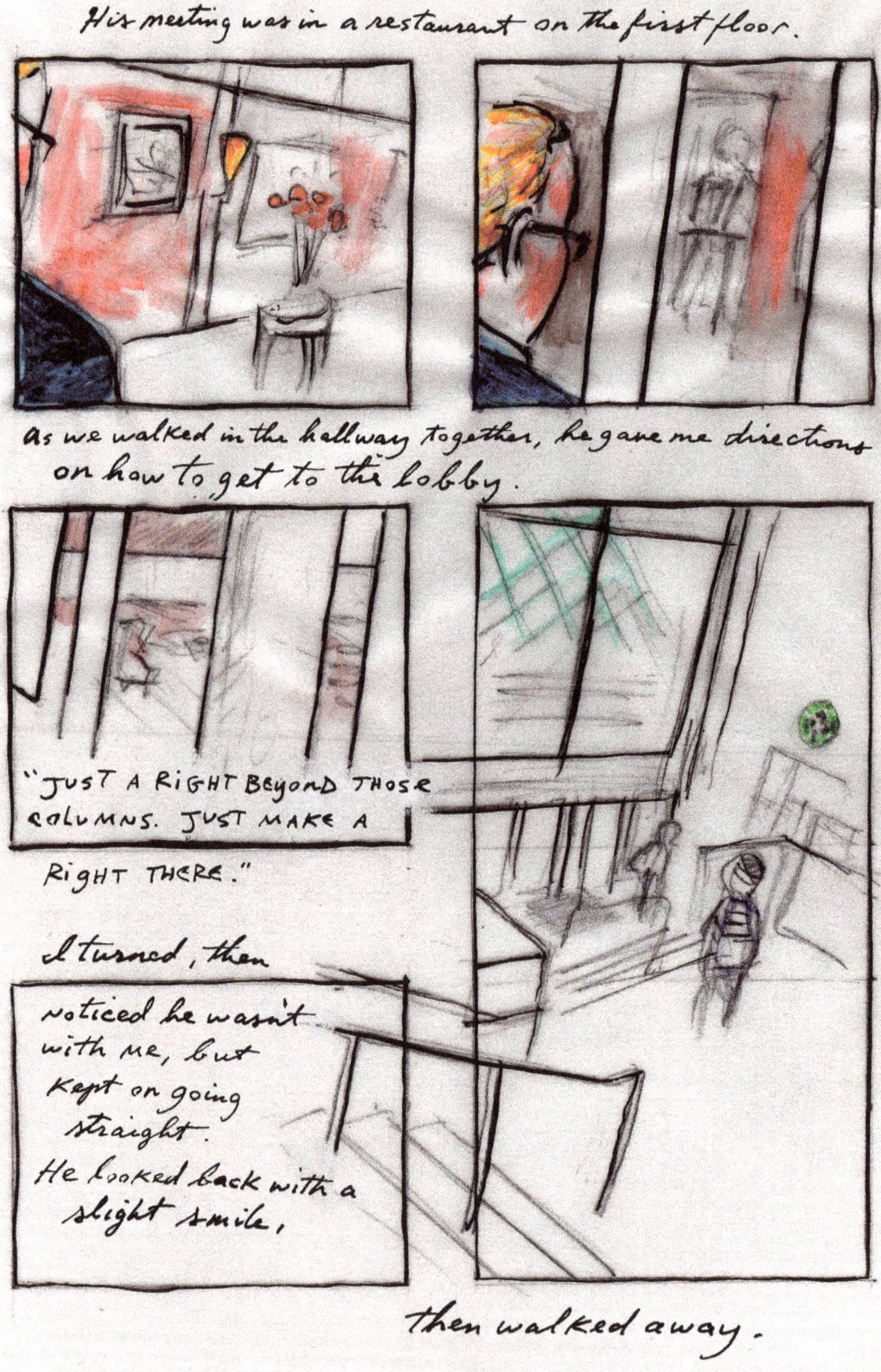

His meeting was in a restaurant on the first floor.

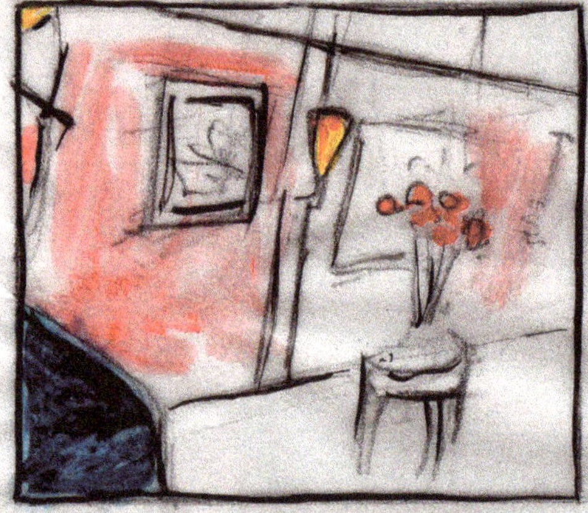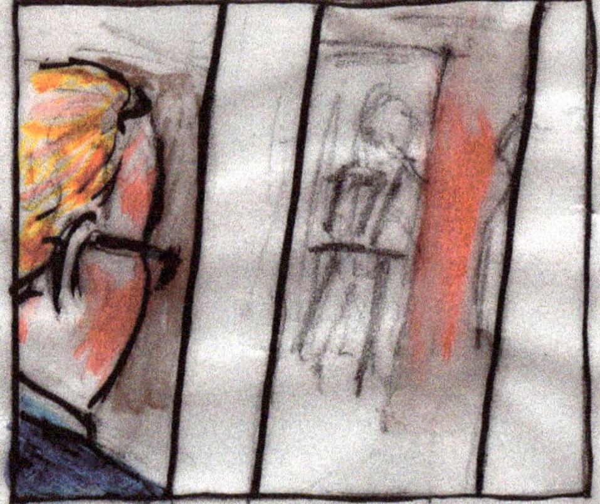

As we walked in the hallway together, he gave me directions on how to get to the lobby.

I turned, then noticed he wasn't with me, but kept on going straight.
He looked back with a slight smile,

then walked away.

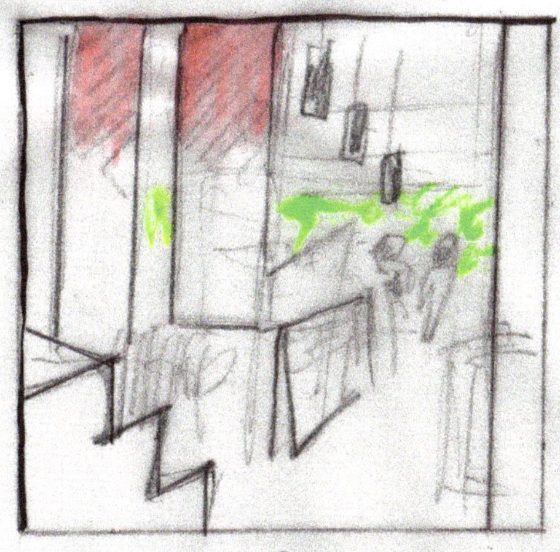
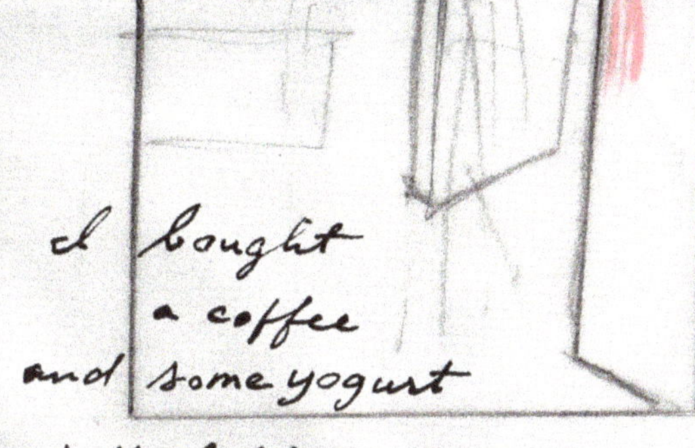

I bought a coffee and some yogurt in the lobby, then plopped down on a couch, slightly numb. Lots of people and families were up and about. Most of the men were sitting, focused on a soccer game on the wide-screen T.V. I watched along with them, feigning interest.

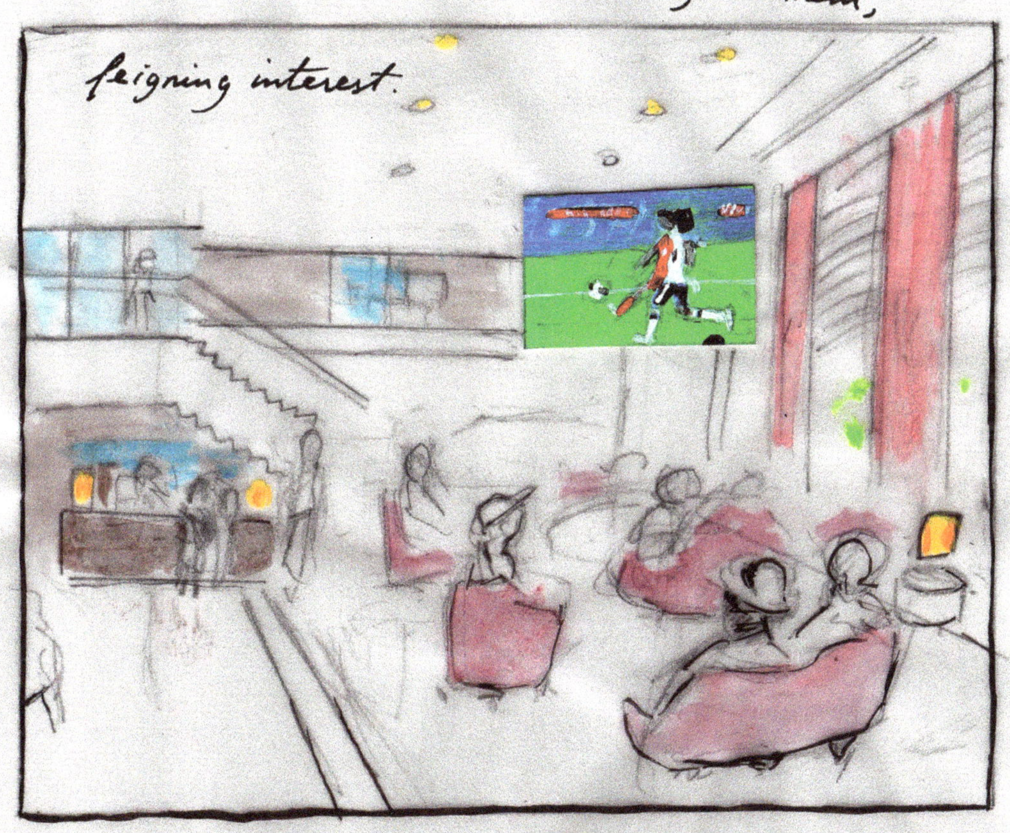

In search of
breakfast, I
walked over to
the pinecrest café.

a well-built
man sat next to me at the counter.
Sharp, Euro-modern glasses, jeans, white t-shirt,
short-cropped hair, tastefully tattooed
muscular biceps.

His up-down-up glance at me said HELLo there,
and so I replied, "Hello."

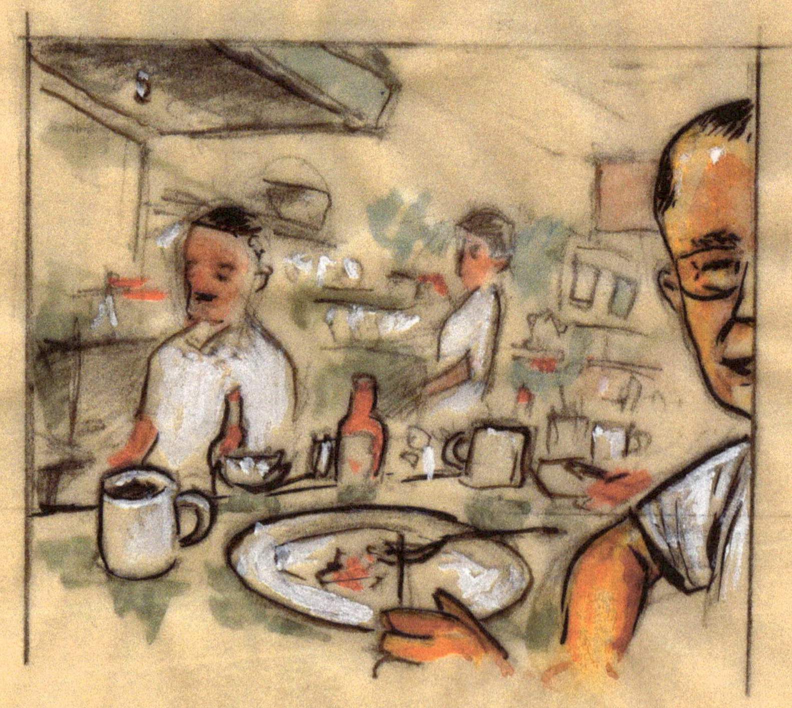

He was the same age as the Baptist. What a contrast, though. `appeared to be very comfortable in his own skin. "BARON" was visiting from Amsterdam. "—for the parade?"
"WELL, NO," he replied, "I'M HERE FOR THE LEATHER PARTIES AT NIGHT. SOMEONE WILL BE TAKING EROTIC PICTURES OF ME
        THIS AFTERNOON."

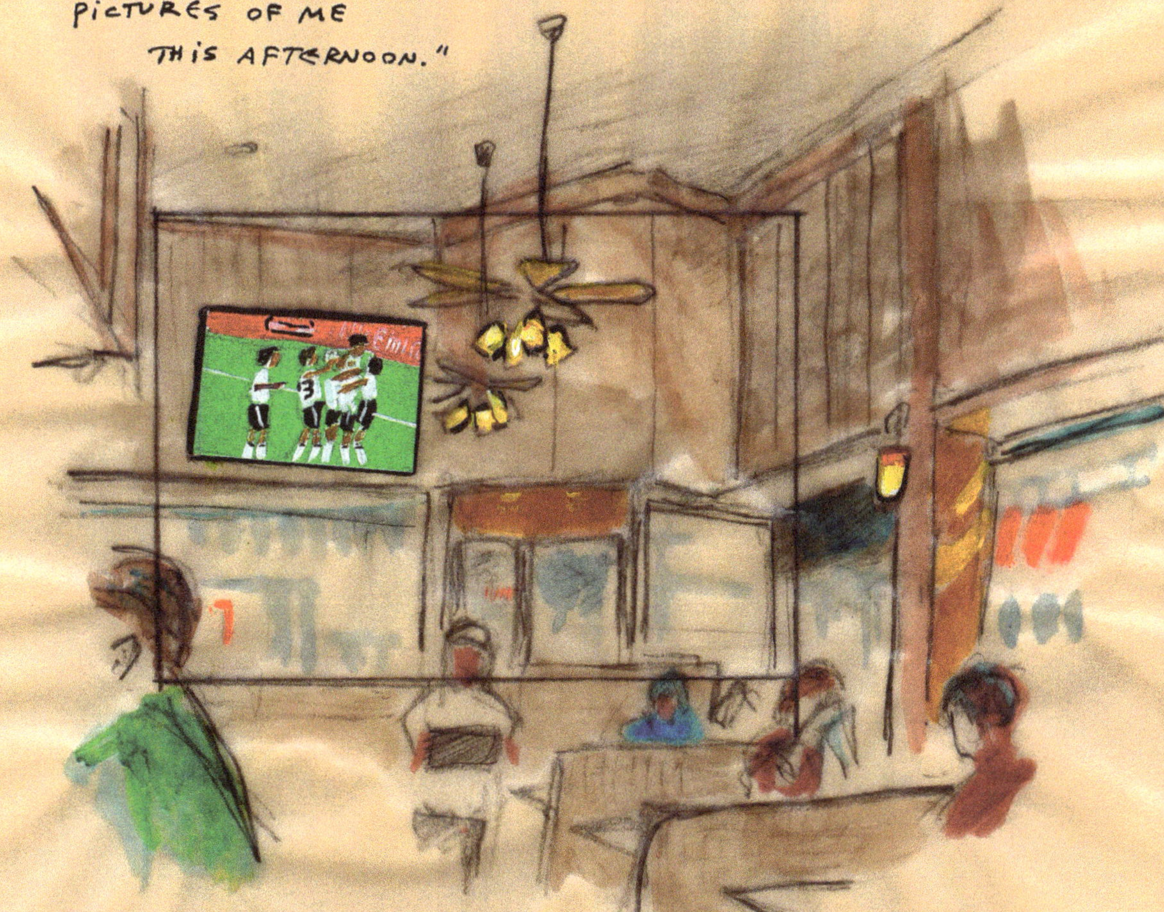

Baron's partner of 20 years was back home— that is, their home in the Florida Keys.
"HE DOESN'T GO FOR THIS SORT OF THING. HE'S BOOKISH —PREFERS CARDIGANS TO LEATHER VESTS. HE KIND OF RESEMBLES YOU."
Did I detect a twinkle in his eye?
He's not a member of any religion.
        "ARE YOU KIDDING ME? NO WAY!
I DON'T GO FOR ANY OF THAT STUFF. IT CAUSES TOO MANY PROBLEMS IN THE WORLD."
We finished our meals and wished each other
    a good day.

I arrived early for the lecture.
the setting was the Fireside Room at
Grace Episcopal Cathedral.
an eclectic assortment of intellectuals gathered.

Father Godfrey, a Jesuit, was discussing
his book about the transformations Most Holy Redeemer
Catholic church experienced as the percentage of
homosexuals in the Castro dramatically increased.

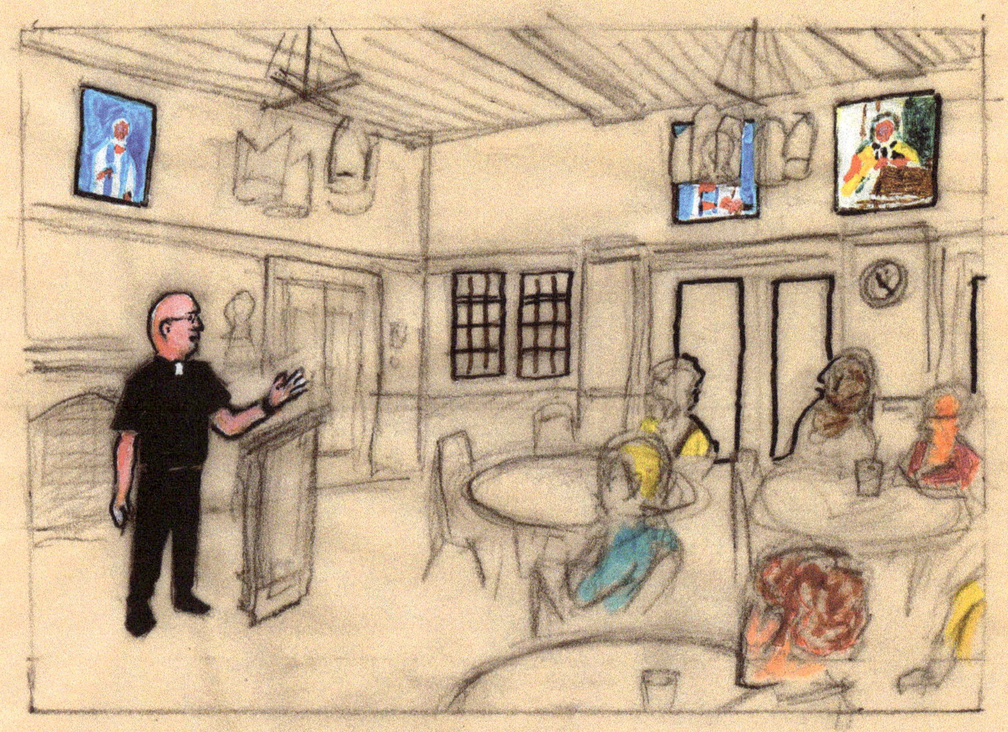

He wrote about former pastor Fr. McGuire
and his viewpoint:

... the Castro is a sacred place. Indeed McGuire's
greatest gift as a pastor was to allow the holiness and
activity of God, already present in the neighborhood,
to come to life again and become manifest
in the parish. and so M.H.R. was renewed
and reborn....

No doubt Godfrey has many enemies,
but I cannot imagine they've ever actually
met the man, for he is as approachable
and compassionate as they come.

Fr. Godfrey said something like,
  "Yes, change in the Church is gradual, I will
agree, and change comes from the ground up.
From the people up to the hierarchy, it is the
parishioners that bring about change."

  A woman brought up a news story from
Rural America, about a gay male who was
found hanging in his garage. On the door,
in spray paint was the phrase **I AM A FAGGOT**

Someone else mentioned the Episcopal church's
openness to gays. Why isn't Father an Anglican?
I pointed out the issue of allowing gays and
lesbians (in relationships) to be ministers is
still threatening to split the Episcopal
church in half.

Afterwards,
  I wandered into the Cathedral proper.
the murals there depict so much history
  and honor so many cultures.

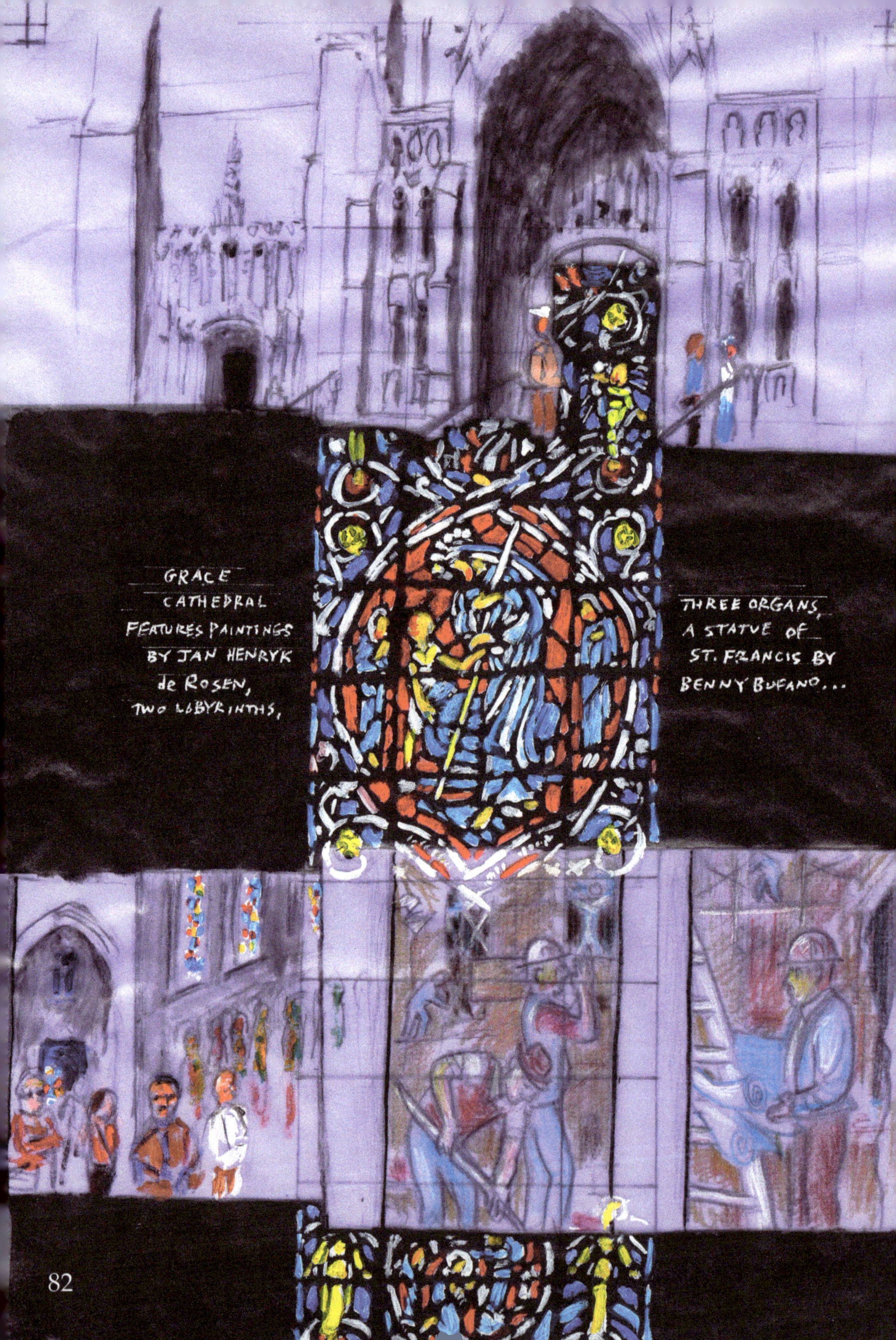

GRACE CATHEDRAL FEATURES PAINTINGS BY JAN HENRYK de ROSEN, TWO LABYRINTHS,
THREE ORGANS, A STATUE OF ST. FRANCIS BY BENNY BUFANO...

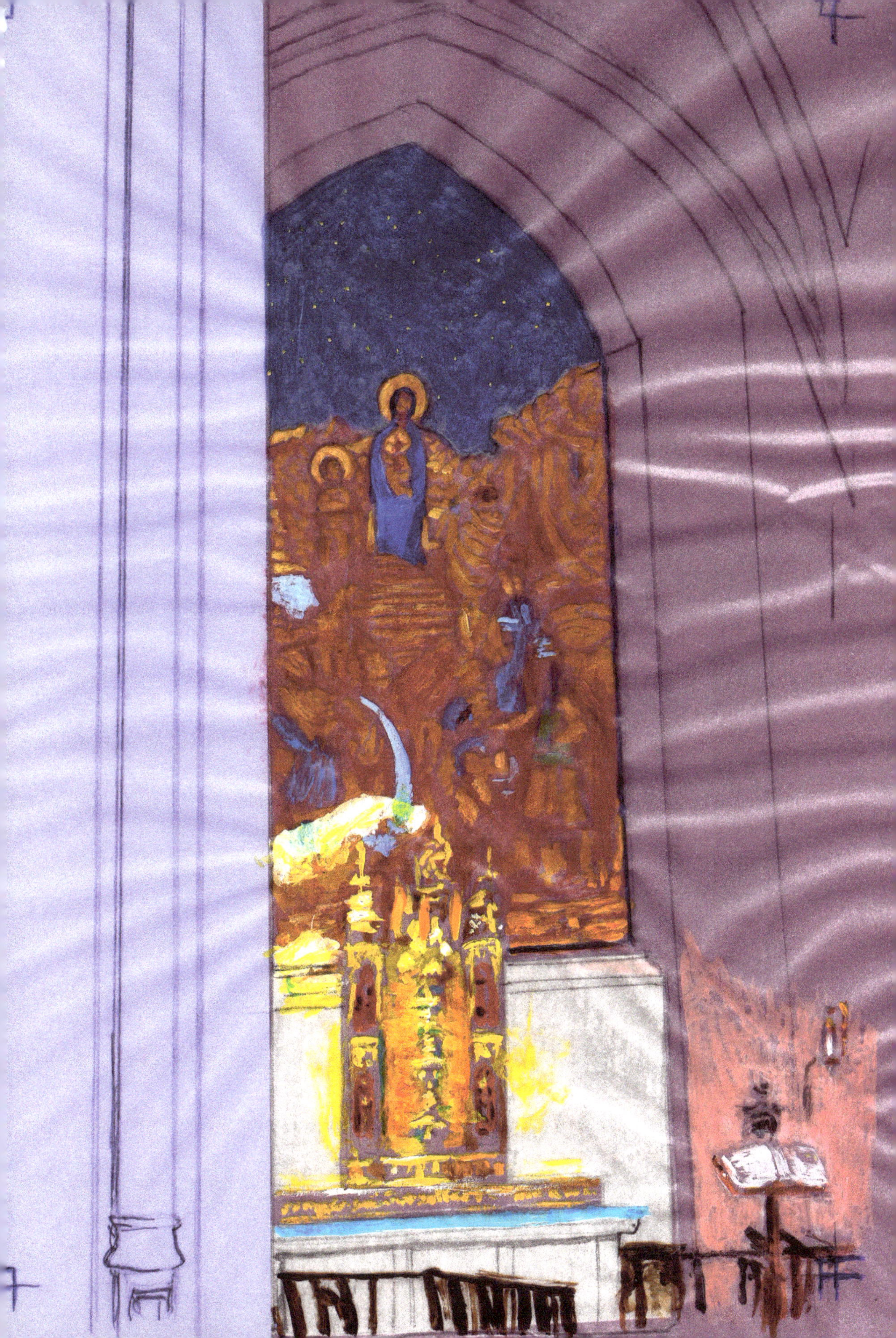

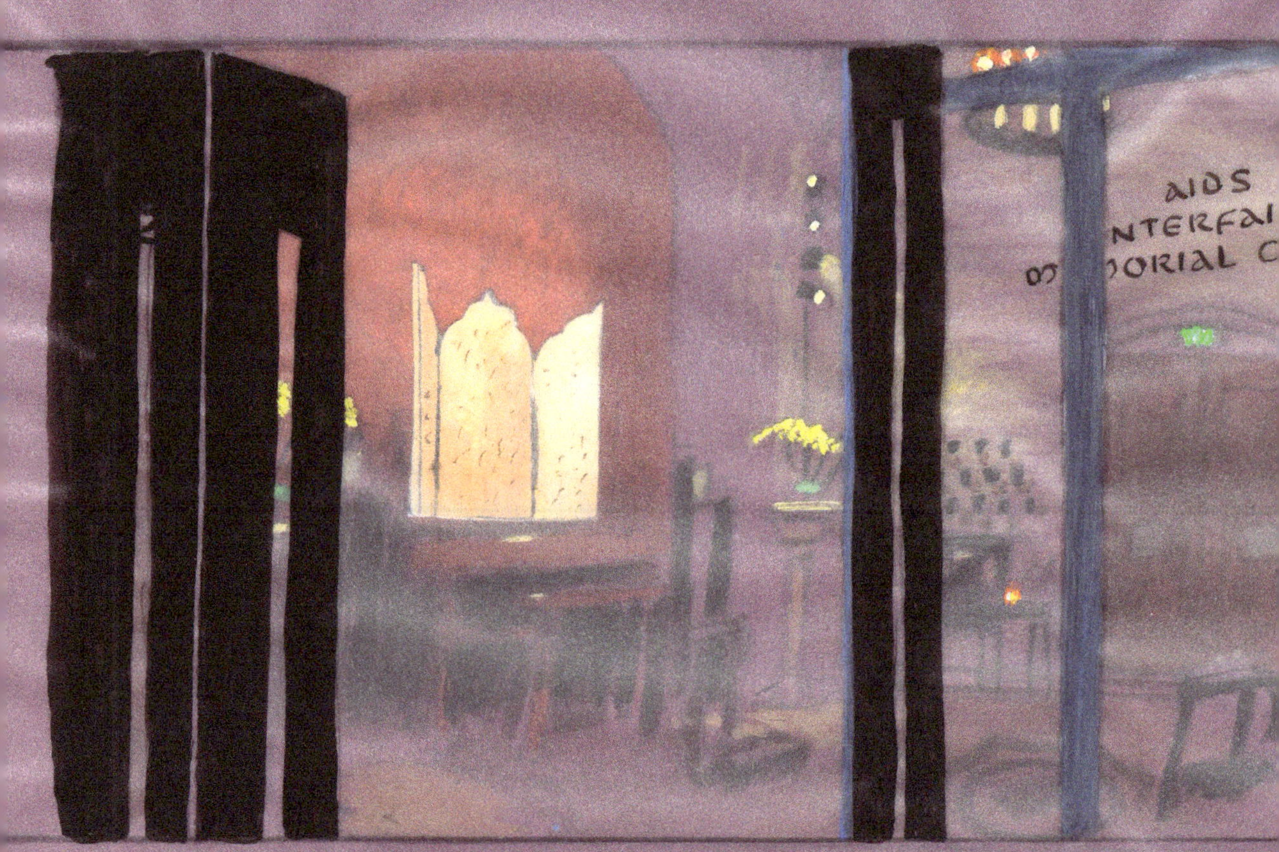

THE AIDS INTERFAITH MEMORIAL CHAPEL.

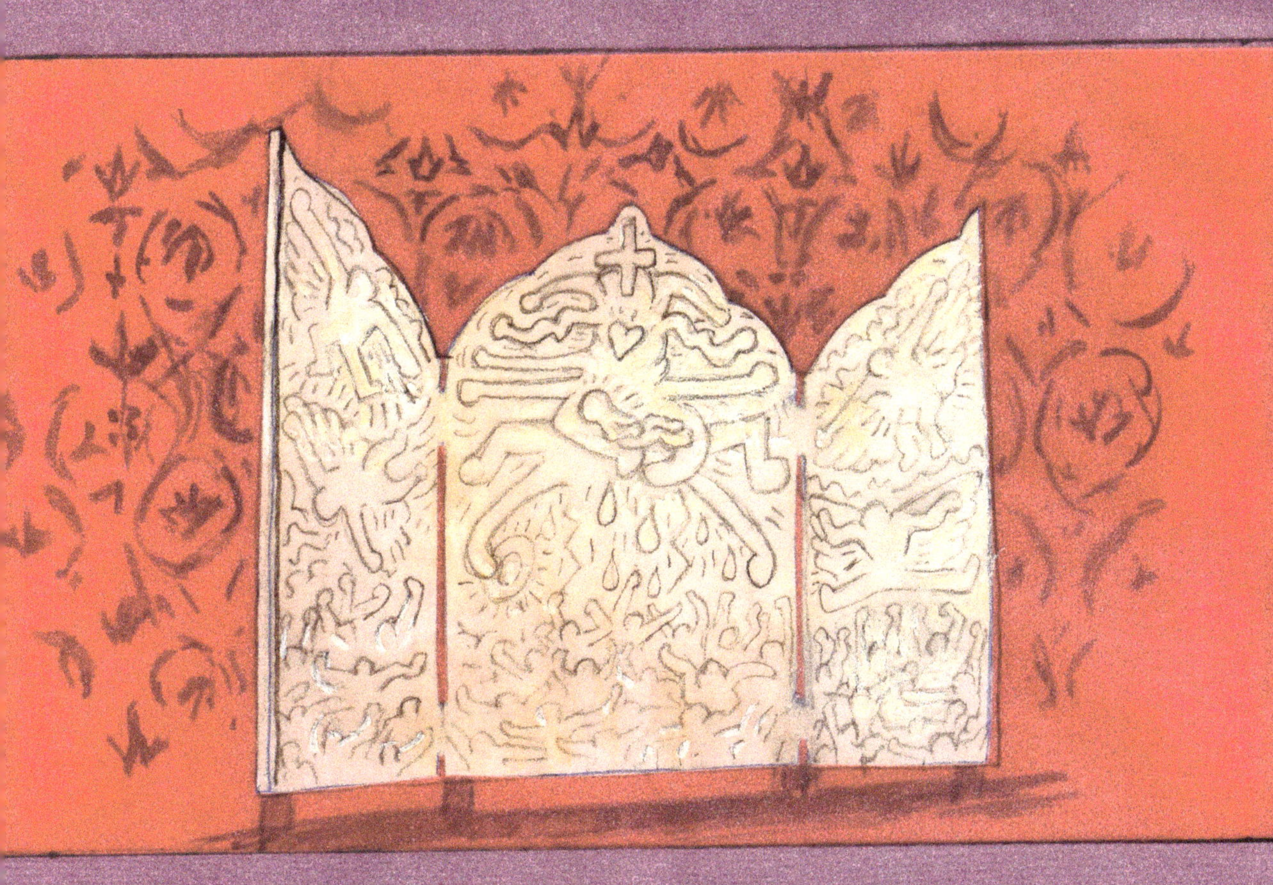

ALTARPIECE BY KEITH HARING.

By now the Pride parade had been going
on for an hour,

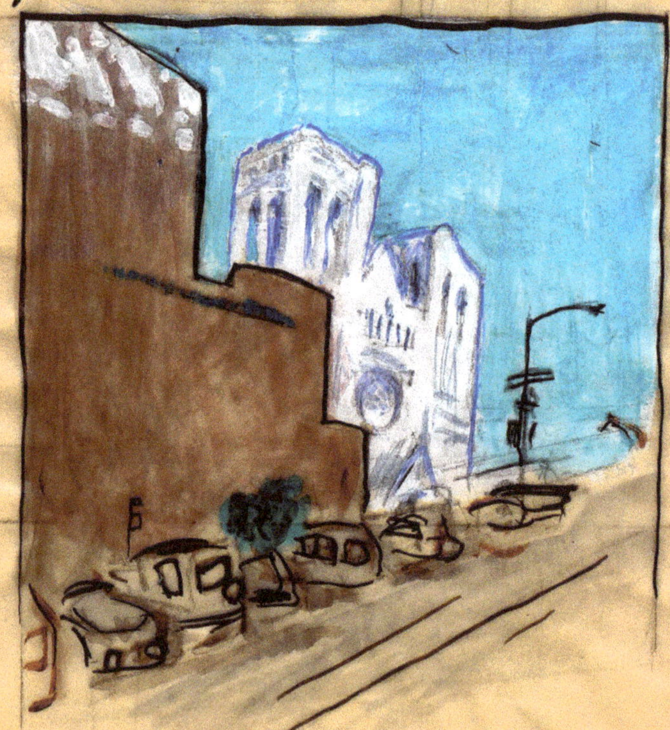

So I headed
down the hill to be one
with the masses.
I can still see it now.
The air is crisp and the
sky is clear.

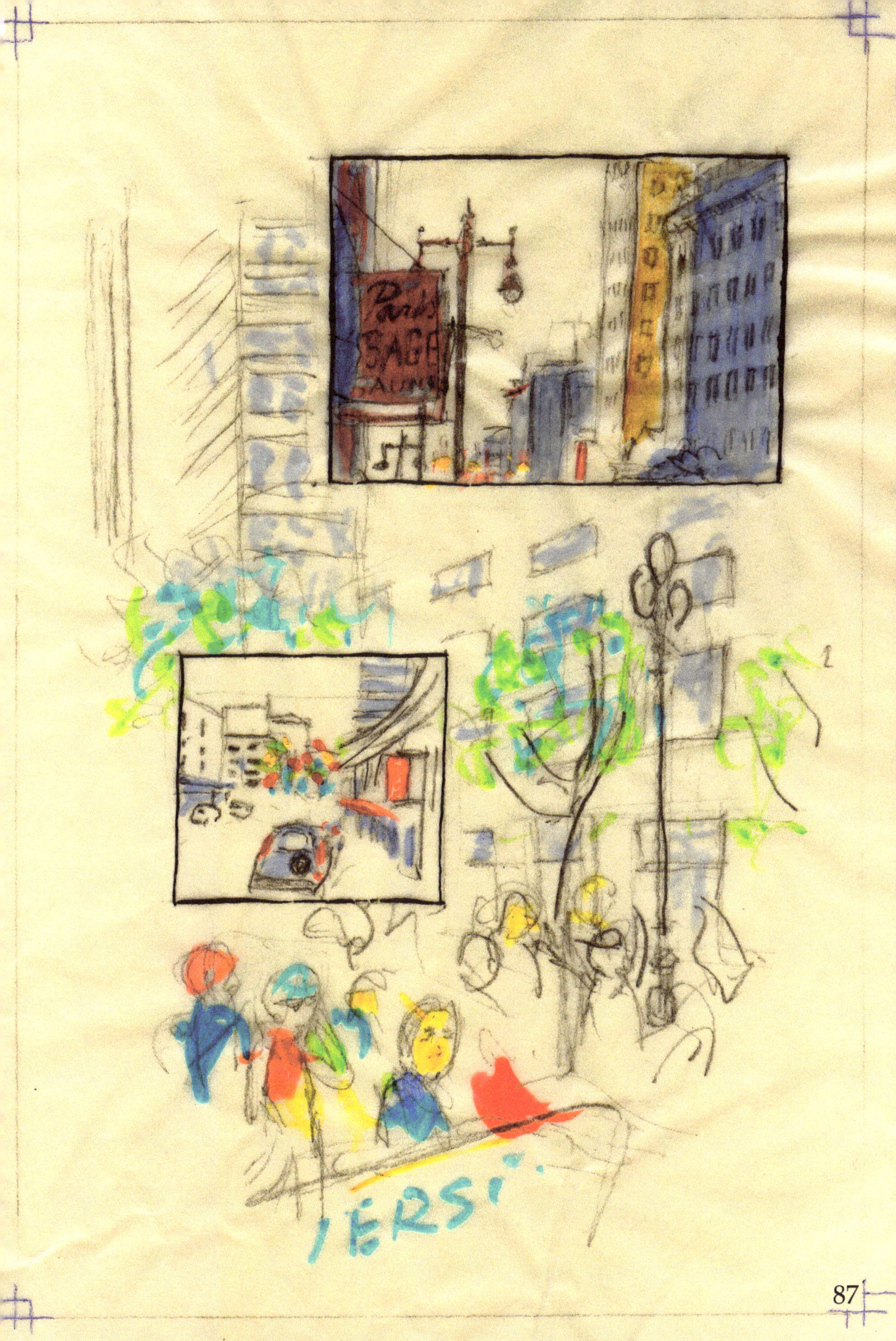
Paris
SAGE
LAUN
IERSI

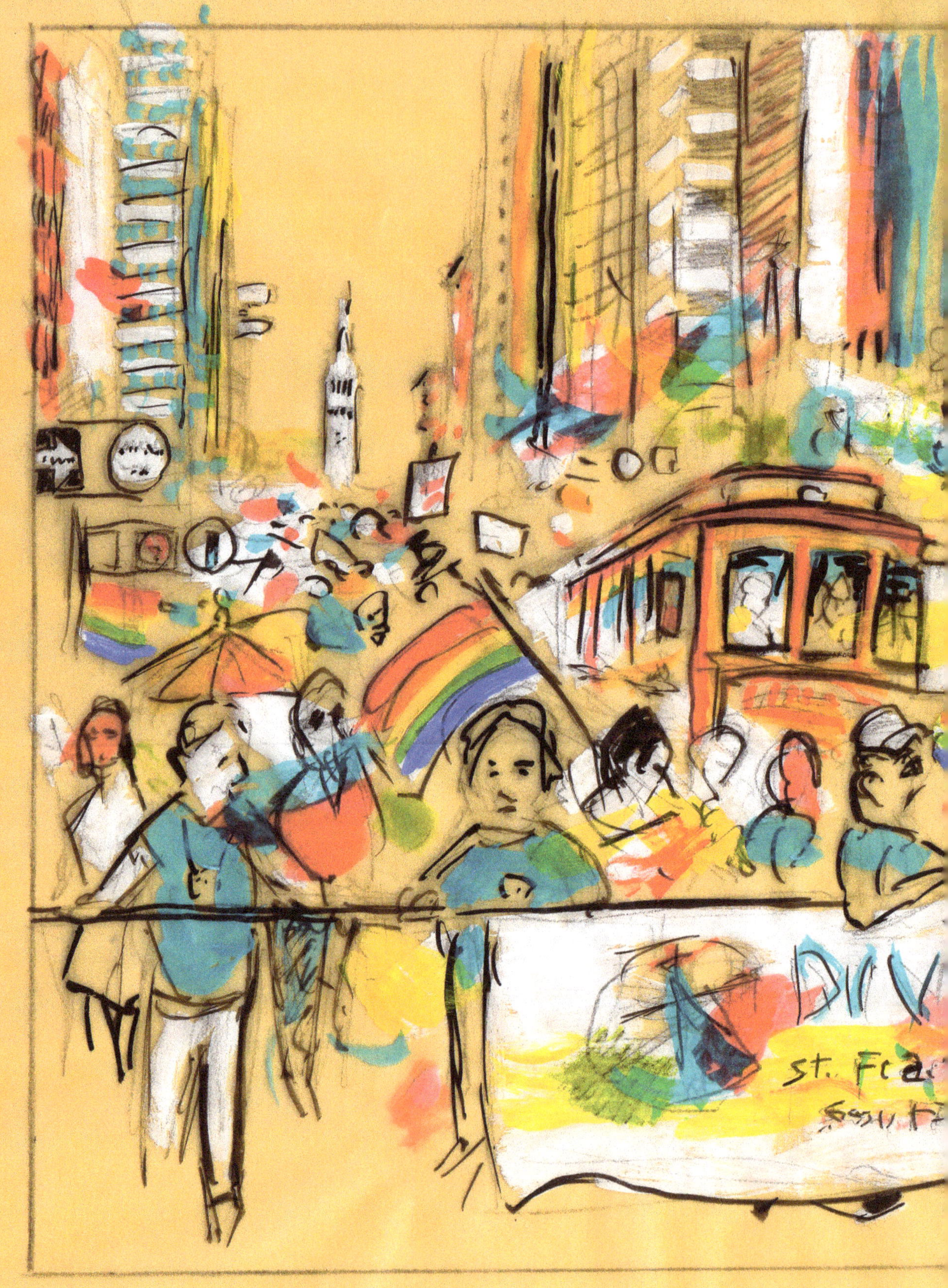

The people are full of life, cheering at
every float, group and band.

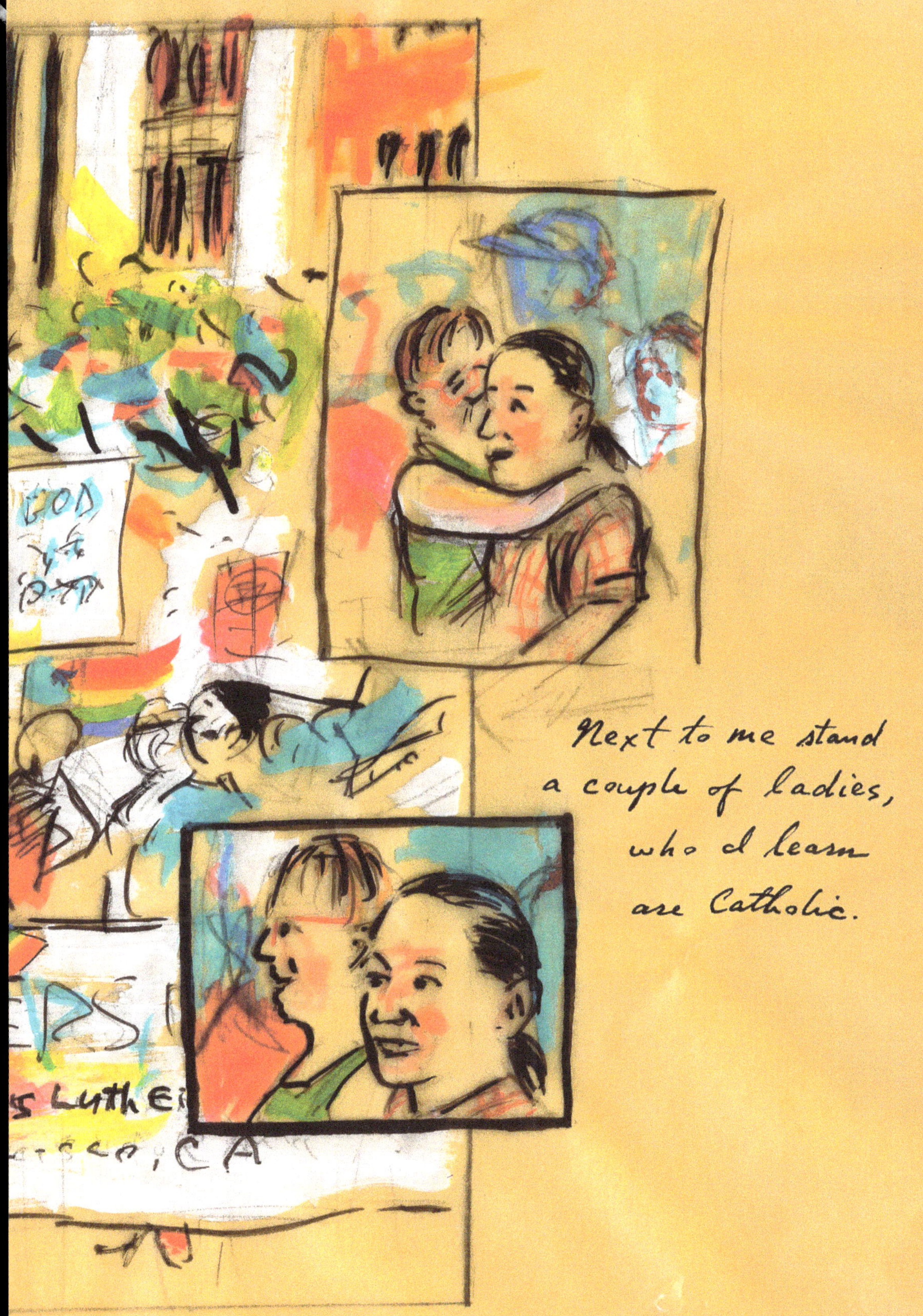

Next to me stand
a couple of ladies,
who I learn
are Catholic.

Several religious Contingents pass by
and the couple smiles.

They cheer,
        they wave,

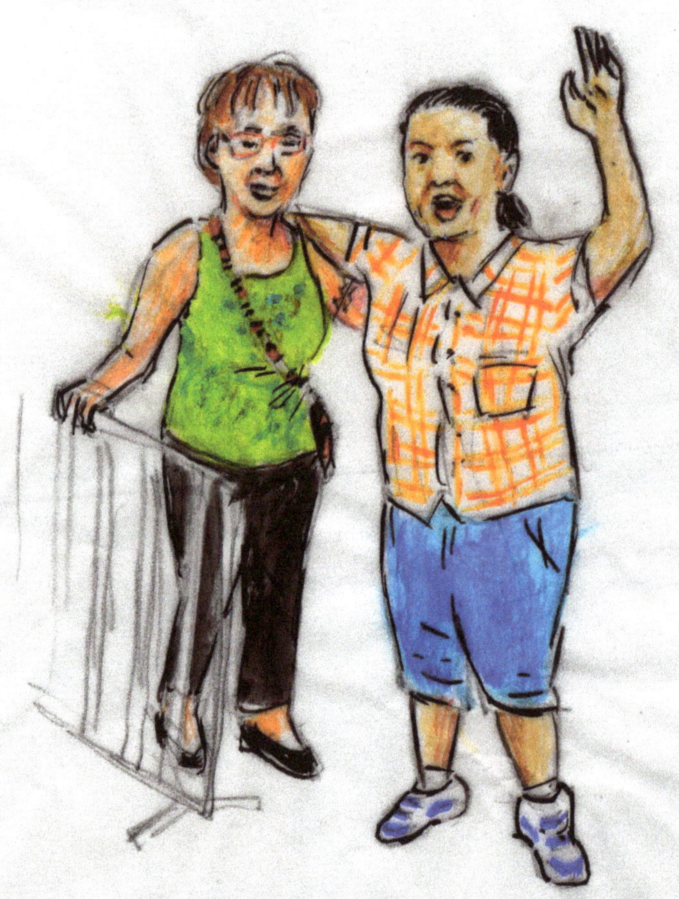

they're happy

and they love each
        other.